Table of Contents

Inquiry-Based Learning: Lessons from Library Power

Jean Donham, PhD
Cornell College

Kay Bishop, PhD
University of South Florida

Carol Collier Kuhlthau, PhD
Rutgers University

Dianne Oberg, PhD
University of Alberta

Linworth Publishing, Inc.

Library of Congress Cataloging-in-Publication Data

Inquiry-based learning: lessons from Library Power/Jean Donham...[et al.].
     p. cm.
   Includes bibliographical references and index.
   ISBN 1-58683-031-7
     1. Library Power (Program)—Case studies. 2. School libraries—United States—Case studies. 3. Instructional materials centers—United States—Case studies. 4. Media programs (Education)—United States—Case studies. 5. Educational change—United States—Case studies. 6. Libraries and education—United States—Case studies. I. Donham, Jean.

Z675.S3 I435 2001
027.8—dc21

2001029881

Published by Linworth Publishing, Inc.
480 East Wilson Bridge Road, Suite L
Worthington, Ohio 43085

Copyright © 2001 by Jean Donham, Kay Bishop, Carol Collier Kuhlthau and Dianne Oberg.

ISBN 1-58683-031-7

5 4 3 2 1

Acknowledgements

The authors would like to thank the library media specialists, administrators, students, and faculty members in the Library Power schools where the case studies took place. Without their cooperation and willingness to welcome the researchers into their school settings, these case studies could not have been reported.

We also extend our appreciation to Jennifer Sprague, who created the index, and to Dr. Jane Bandy Smith and Dr. Julie Tallman, who offered insightful and beneficial review comments during the development of this book.

Introduction

In 1988, the DeWitt Wallace Reader's Digest Fund provided funds to schools in New York City as the first Library Power projects. This was the beginning of a ten-year program of funding school library programs. This multi-million-dollar initiative coincided with the publication of *Information Power*, the 1988 guidelines for school libraries, generated jointly by the American Association of School Librarians and the Association for Educational Communications and Technology. Over time, nineteen communities received three-year grants of $1.2 million each. Each community developed its own plan for improving its school library program and determined the way in which the school library would improve student performance. All participating schools agreed to provide a full-time librarian, funds for collection development, and open access to the library throughout the school day. They also agreed to support collaborative planning for teachers and librarians to work together throughout the school year. The University of Wisconsin was appointed to evaluate the results of the Library Power program, with Dianne McAfee Hopkins and Douglas Zweizig as co-directors of the evaluation process. They, in turn, identified case study researchers to engage in description and analysis of the activities of participating schools. As preliminary data emerged from case studies, the evaluation process expanded to include thematic studies of selected schools. First-year observations in three selected schools revealed evidence of a transition toward inquiry-based learning. Carol Collier Kuhlthau (1999) analyzed the findings from these schools to characterize this change. This book reports the findings of these three studies in schools where the Library Power initiative had facilitated a move toward an inquiry approach to teaching and learning.

This book tells the stories of three schools where library media programs played an instrumental role in curriculum renewal. The schools have in common the fundamental tenets of the Library Power initiative: improved collections, flexible access to the library media center, and a collaborative approach to using library resources in instruction. Beyond those three characteristics, these schools also have in common a commitment to inquiry-based teaching and learning. In all three schools, case researchers observed students using the library media center to seek information. In these schools, teachers, principals, and librarians worked together to engage children in learning—encouraging them to be inquirers, helping them to internalize an information-seeking process, and sustaining the sense of wonder that children bring to school. The stories of these schools can guide others to create schools where curiosity and inquiry characterize the children who attend and where school libraries are alive with children seeking answers to their questions or information that leads to further questions.

Why is inquiry-based learning important? Simply stated, it is the way we learn in "real life." As adults, we continue to learn as long as we continue to wonder, ask questions, and inquire. For students to go through school learning only how to answer the questions that teachers ask but not learning how to generate their own questions and develop strategies for answering them fails to prepare them for real life. We know that children come to school full of wonder and questions, but traditional schools quickly turn off that sense of wonder and question-asking and turn children into answer-seekers. For children to own their learning, they need to own their questions. Inquiry-based learning is a deep and fundamental change for most American schools. It requires a change in role for the teacher and the student. It changes the approach to curriculum. It adjusts the focus of instruction toward learning processes as well as content. School librarians have a potential role to play as facilitators of this shift, as teachers who develop in students the skills and knowledge to be inquirers, and as collaborators with teachers in re-designing curriculum and instruction to address the inquiry process in the context of content learning.

Too often the gap between research and practice is wide. Researchers collect data, analyze it, and develop and test theories. Yet, their findings fail to reach practitioners who could improve practice based on the insights research provides. By bringing together theory, principles, and concrete examples, the authors hope to present research in such a way that it will truly inform practice, assist practitioners in envisioning the transformation that inquiry-based learning represents, and support the application of *what we know* from research to *what we do* in schools.

Chapter 1 will explore further the need for an inquiry approach to teaching and learning. It will provide the foundation for the cases described. In it, Carol Collier Kuhlthau will define inquiry-based learning. She will provide its theoretical underpinnings in what we know about how children learn, and she will differentiate it from other approaches to the teaching and learning processes. In Chapters 2, 3, and 4, Library Power case researchers will describe individual schools. In each case, the author will describe learning situations in the school, explain how teachers, administrators and librarians worked together, and describe the inquiry-based learning in the school. Each of these case studies revealed one particular feature that supported inquiry-based learning. These features were adoption of an information search process model, teacher transformation, and information resources. The chapters describing each of these cases will emphasize these features.

Chapter 2 focuses on adoption of a model of the research process. This chapter describes an elementary school where faculty and the library media specialist work collaboratively to incorporate an information search process into the school's curriculum. All teachers and the library media specialist have adopted the process model and teach the process using consistent language and expectations. This chapter explores the ways in which the model enhances communication among teachers and creates consistency between classrooms and the library media center. The model guides instruction, student assessment, and curriculum development.

Chapter 3 characterizes the teacher transformation at the heart of inquiry-based learning. Teachers (including library media specialists and principals) must develop a personal understanding of the constructivist theory that underpins inquiry-based learning. For many educators, this means more than learning something new; it means transforming their deeply held beliefs and practices. The case described in Chapter 3 illustrates the important distinction between structural and normative change. True reform demands not only changes in the school's structure but, more important perhaps, changes in the norms of teacher and student beliefs about teaching and learning and subsequent changes in the activities of the teaching and learning processes.

Chapter 4 explores the importance of information resources relevant to the topics. The mix of people and resources necessary to implement inquiry-based learning is fragile. When students pose questions, the breadth and depth of available resources must increase to accommodate their individual needs. Likewise, physical facilities must support increased use of the library media center by various groups throughout the school day. Observing what happens when any of those elements change emphasizes the importance of these contextual factors. Each of the cases ends with a list of "lessons learned" from this school—practical steps that schools can take to move toward more emphasis on student-driven inquiry.

A concluding chapter brings together the findings of the three cases and identifies the common ground among them in an effort to guide schools seeking to become inquiry-based schools.

Appendixes describe the research methodology used in the case studies, portray scenarios to provide an image of inquiry-based learning in these schools, suggest open-ended organizers useful in assisting children in the inquiry process, provide suggestions for further reading, and introduce the authors.

For the sake of confidentiality, the schools described in these three cases will be identified by fictitious names.

Reference

Kuhlthau, Carol Collier. "Student learning in the library: What Library Power librarians say." *School Libraries Worldwide 5/2* (July 1999): 80-96.

Chapter 1

Inquiry-Based Learning

Carol Collier Kuhlthau

I nquiry-based learning is an approach to instruction that centers on the research process. This approach, which actively involves students in the process of learning, begins by engaging them in questions about the subject being studied (Harste, 1994; Harste and Callison, 1994). Students are guided through inquiry by asking themselves: What do I already know? What questions do I have? How do I find out? And finally, what did I learn? Inquiry takes students out of the predigested format of the textbook and rote memorization into the process of learning from a variety of sources to construct their own understandings. They learn to think through subject content apart from prescribed responses or preset solutions. They are guided through a process of intellectual construction that enables them to build on what they already know and to come to a deeper understanding of the concepts and problems underlying the subject. Library Power seems to have the most significant influence on student learning in those schools where it is tied to other reform efforts that are directing schools to a constructivist approach to learning centering on inquiry in the research process.

Constructivist Theory of Learning

The constructivist theory of learning focuses on the process of thinking that builds understandings by engaging students in stimulating encounters with information and ideas. Students learn by constructing their own understandings of these experiences and by building on what they already know to form a personal perspective of the world. The process of construction is an active ongoing process of learning that continues throughout life. Continuity between the curriculum and instruction within the school and the child's own experiences outside the school promotes sustained meaningful learning. As the school reform team from the University of Wisconsin-Madison discovered, learning improves where students are constructing knowledge through guided inquiry that has value beyond the school (Neumann, 1995). Authentic learning involves instruction and assessment that provides connections between the school and the outside world. Inquiry-based learning is an effective way for students to engage in authentic learning across the curriculum.

While many library media programs are more in line with a transmission approach to learning that emphasizes finding the right answer, memorizing specific facts, and repackaging information, inquiry-based learning calls for thinking and reflecting in the process of information seeking. Models that emphasize structuring instruction to transmit specific facts and skills are not inquiry models. Inquiry-based learning is grounded in a constructivist foundation that views learning as an active, continuing process of constructing knowledge that has meaning and value in one's own life.

Educational Concepts about How Children Learn

Over the past ten years, the constructivist approach to learning has been a particularly useful theoretical foundation for reforming schools. Constructivist theory also has been developing as a theoretical foundation for restructuring the library media center program in order to meet the challenges of the information-age school. The framework for this theory includes some primary concepts drawn from educational research that are based on what we know about how children learn.

■ **Children learn by being actively engaged and reflecting on that experience.**

Constructivists view learning as an active, engaging process in which all aspects of experience are called into play. In the first half of the twentieth century, John Dewey (1944), an early constructivist, articulated a philosophy of education for a democratic state that would prepare students for work, citizenship, and life in a free society. Dewey (1933) described learning as an active individual process—something that a person does, not something done to someone. "Education is not an affair of telling and being told but an active constructive process." Learning takes place through a combination of acting and reflecting on the consequences, what Dewey called reflective experience or reflective thinking. Activity is only half the story; it is in the reflection on the activity that constructive learning takes place.

More recently, Jerome Bruner's (1973) studies of perception and his later writings (1990) expanded on the constructivist view of the nature of human thinking and learning. Bruner's research confirmed that people who are actively involved in making sense of the world rather than passive receivers of information learn best. He explained that it is not enough to merely gather information. Learning involves "going beyond the information given" to create "products of mind." These concepts and theories are discussed more fully in *Seeking Meaning: A Process Approach to Library and Information Services* (Kuhlthau, 1993).

■ **Children learn by building on what they already know.**

One of the basic tenets of constructivist theory is that past experience and prior understandings form the basis for constructing new knowledge. Widely accepted as a foundation of education, "schema theory" is the development of this concept. Kelly (1963), Piaget (Elkind, 1976), and Bartlett (1932) are major theorists in this area. They, along with many others, have provided an extensive body of literature on how children build schema or constructs that form their view of the world. The central concept of these theorists is that connections to a child's present knowledge are essential for constructing new understandings.

■ **Children develop higher-order thinking through guidance at critical points in the learning process.**

The concept of higher-order thinking, as explored and explained by Vygotsky (1978), is an important element of constructivist theory. Higher-order thinking entails deep processing that leads to understanding. Unfortunately, most schoolwork is limited to shallow processing in response to simple or superficial questions with prescribed answers. Deep processing requires engagement and motivation fostered by authentic questions that stimulate inquiry within a constructivist approach to learning.

Building on Vygotsky's concept, we can think of teaching as organizing the learning environment so that children are confronted with authentic questions drawn from their own experience and curiosity. Schools need to provide resources for students to explore questions, with guidance at critical points in the learning process. Borrowing from Vygotsky's concept of a zone of proximal development, we can develop guidance around a "zone of intervention," in which a student can do with advice and assistance what he or she cannot do alone or can do only with great difficulty (Kuhlthau, 1993). Teachers and library media specialists who are able to recognize those critical moments when intervention and instruction are essential can tailor interventions to enable children to achieve understanding in the learning process.

■ **Children's development occurs in a sequence of stages.**

Constructivists recognize and respect cognitive development as an important consideration in learning. Piaget (Elkind, 1976) describes children as progressing through stages of cognitive development, with their capacity for abstract thinking increasing with age. The young thinker may have difficulty dealing with the more abstract aspects of inquiry. Since the research process requires considerable abstraction, there is a need to accommodate inquiry tasks to the child's level of cognitive development. Inquiry-based learning can be effectively designed for learning in each stage of cognitive development.

In pre-kindergarten through fifth grade, inquiry-based learning involves children in asking questions, seeking answers, and sharing their discoveries with others. Children in fifth through eighth grades are in a stage of transition toward more abstraction in learning. These students explore ideas from various sources and integrate those ideas into their own thinking. They are preparing for forming a focused perspective within the process of information seeking that they can develop for sharing and applying (Kuhlthau, 1994).

■ **Children have different ways of learning.**

Constructivist theory portrays learning as a holistic experience with many ways of knowing. Children learn through all of their senses. They apply all of their physical, mental, and social capabilities. The notion of a set learning style is giving way to the concept of multiple intelligences developed by Howard Gardner (1983). A wide range of resources in an array of formats presented through a variety of activities offers children a wealth of opportunities for learning. Reading, listening, viewing, and observing are joined with writing, speaking, performing, and producing for encompassing the holistic experience of learning. Inquiry-based learning offers many ways to construct deep understandings of the world and one's life in it.

■ **Children learn through social interaction with others.**

Children are constantly learning through interaction with others around them. The experience of learning through interaction is called social construction. Children construct their understandings of the world through continuous, ongoing interaction with the people in their lives. Parents, peers, siblings, teachers, acquaintances, and strangers are all part of the social environment that forms a learning environment in which children are continuously constructing and making meaning for themselves.

Drawn from educational research, these six primary concepts about how children learn form a foundation for a constructivist theory of learning. They support the adoption of inquiry as a way of learning across the curriculum in the information-age school.

Learning in Information-Rich Environments

An information-age school engages students in learning in an information-rich environment. Accordingly, school library media specialists can make a major contribution toward restructuring schools for this engagement by providing opportunities for children to learn and to develop an understanding of learning in these information-rich environments. Some basic concepts from information science research offer insight into the process of information seeking and have important implications for children in the inquiry process.

Library and information science research reveals that people engage in information seeking in order to find meaning, not merely to locate information. People experience different stages in the process of information seeking, and their information need changes and evolves as they learn more. Research reveals that people have difficulty expressing what they need in the early stages of information seeking, but once they are able to express their need, they are close to resolving the situation that initially prompted their search for information. In a similar pattern, people in the workplace confront complex tasks that require considerable learning and constructing, and frequently these tasks require an extensive search for information over an extended period of time. Complex tasks create considerable uncertainty in the early stages, but there is evidence that these complex tasks lead to more innovative and value-added contributions to the work of the individual or organization. These findings about people using information in their work reveal the importance of learning to construct knowledge from a variety of sources of information.

Stages in the Inquiry Process

In school library media centers, the process of inquiry has been extensively studied and modeled as the Information Search Process (ISP). Research has centered on investigating the student's perspective of the inquiry process as a way of constructing knowledge. My own research in this area was initiated in the mid-1980s with a qualitative study of high school students, revealing their thoughts, actions, and feelings in a sequence of stages in the research process. Since then, the stages of the ISP have been verified in a series of studies applying both qualitative and quantitative methods and incorporating longitudinal and large-scale design with a variety of participants. Full descriptions of the studies and of the model of the stages in the ISP have been provided in prior publications (Kuhlthau, 1993).

Kuhlthau's Information Search Process Model includes not only this cognitive aspect of the search process but also the affective aspect of information searching.

The ISP involves seven stages: Initiation, Selection, Exploration, Formulation, Collection, Presentation, and Assessment. These stages are named for the primary task to be accomplished at each point in the process. The first stage, Initiation, occurs when the teacher announces an invitation to research an engaging question, designed to motivate students to undertake the inquiry process. This comprehensive engaging question is developed by the teacher and library media specialist from the instructional goals and standards of the curriculum. The task of students in this stage is to contemplate the question and the accompanying assignment in preparation for the investigation ahead. The second stage is Selection, in which students choose what to pursue in response to the initiating question by considering what they already know and what they want and need to find out. In the third stage, Exploration, students explore the initiating question and develop questions of their own that arise as they begin to learn about the subject. Exploration is the most difficult stage of the ISP when students commonly encounter information that is inconsistent and incompatible with what they already know and what they expect to find. In all three of the beginning stages of the ISP, students often experience confusion, uncertainty, and apprehension. The fourth stage is Formulation, in which students become aware of the various dimensions, issues, and ramifications of the initiating question and begin to form their own focused perspective of the subject under study. During the fifth stage, which is Collection, students gather information that defines, extends, and supports the focus that they have formed. During Collection, their interest and confidence commonly increases as they gain a sense of ownership and expertise in the subject. The sixth stage is Presentation—preparing to share what has been learned with the others in the learning community. In the seventh stage, Assessment, students reflect on what they have learned and discover what went well and what might be improved.

The ISP model describes the thoughts, actions, and feelings commonly experienced by students in each stage of the inquiry process. The feelings of students while they are engaged in an inquiry project reveal much about the learning process they are experiencing and the interventions they need. In the early stages, making connections with what they already know and forming questions about what they don't know facilitates initiating and selecting. This lays the groundwork for exploring and formulating in the critical middle stages of the learning process. Unfortunately, in school assignments, the early stages are often hurried, and the middle stages are frequently passed over as students are urged to collect and complete their work. The inquiry process is a thinking process that requires extensive exploration of ideas and formulation of thoughts before moving on to the later stages of collecting and preparing to present. At completion, when assessing the inquiry process, students often find that they missed the critical stages of learning by not allowing time for reflecting and formulating while they were exploring and collecting information.

This insight into the process of learning from a variety of sources of information forms the basis for guiding students in the inquiry process and for developing a program of inquiry-based learning. Taken together, the primary concepts drawn from educational research of how children learn and the basic concepts from library and information science research about how people search for information offer a substantial constructivist theory of learning that supports the implementation of inquiry-based learning.

Library Media Specialists' Perceptions of Learning

Library media specialists have opinions, beliefs, and theories that shape their actions, and those theories shape the library media programs they implement in their schools. Perceptions of what constitutes learning form the theory that underlies the library media programs provided for students. It is important to reflect on what assumptions are made about learning in the library. What do we emphasize? What do we expect? What do we reward? The Library Power evaluation project offered an opportunity to study library media specialists' perceptions of learning over a three-year period of involvement in the Library Power initiative (Kuhlthau, 1999). One of the items on the annual survey of participating library media specialists elicited their perceptions of student learning. In each of the three years that the survey was administered, the library media specialists were asked to describe an incident of student learning in the library media center by responding to the following prompt. "Think back over your Library Power program to a time when a student or students had a meaningful learning experience in the library. How did you know something new was learned? What stands out in your mind that made it a good learning experience?"

The first year of the study, the highest number of responses emphasized a positive change in attitude. In the second year, the highest number of responses emphasized competence in information skills. In the third year, the highest number of responses emphasized utilization of information for learning. Over the course of the Library Power program, it became apparent that many library media specialists were changing what they considered important when describing student learning. Early in the initiative, they noted a change in attitude. Next, they stressed competence in locating information and using technology. By the third year, many had turned their attention to using information for learning in the content areas. This progression revealed that many library media specialists had changed their perspectives of learning through participation in the Library Power initiative. Emphasis on utilization of resources for learning is essential for implementing inquiry-based learning in collaboration with teachers.

By the third year of participation in the Library Power initiative, many library media specialists were implementing an inquiry approach to learning in the library media center. Library Power was a school reform initiative that changed the way teachers teach and the way students learn. The roles of teachers, library media specialists, and students were transformed in these schools. Teachers and library media specialists worked together to engage students in using a variety of resources for learning and to guide students through the process of inquiry-based learning. Teachers developed engaging questions based on curriculum standards to initiate the inquiry process, and library media specialists provided a wide range of resources based on the curriculum that were essential for learning through the inquiry process. However, the students played a critical role by taking an active role in their own learning. The case studies in this book describe student learning in three schools that were selected as places that emphasized utilization of resources for learning where students were actively involved in inquiry-based learning.

Implementing Inquiry-Based Learning

Inquiry-based learning enables students to meaningfully accomplish the objectives of the curriculum by preparing them for living and learning in the world outside of the school. The library media specialist and the teacher form a team to implement inquiry-based learning in the content areas of the curriculum. The collaboration is not a duplication of effort; it brings together essential elements that neither partner can fully provide alone. The library media specialist provides the resources and the process, and the teacher provides the content and the context. The case studies in this book offer numerous examples of collaboration that combine the expertise of the teacher and the library media specialist to achieve curriculum objectives through an inquiry-based approach.

Strategies for implementing inquiry in the elementary school need to accommodate the stages of cognitive development of children in the early grades where they are developing abilities that they will build on in the later grades. At the earliest ages, we can help children begin to develop the basics of inquiry by asking them to recall, summarize, and paraphrase, and to extend so as to construct their own understandings (Kuhlthau, 1993). Recalling is prompted by simply asking, "What do you remember?" Summarizing is encouraged by asking students, "What parts do you want to tell?" and then guiding them not to tell everything but to select what to tell. Paraphrasing values children's telling by encouraging them to "tell in your own words." Children can be led to extend by giving them opportunities to tell: "What else do you know? What more do you want to know?"

The constructivist view of learning fosters practical strategies for implementing inquiry-based learning. Such strategies build on what children know, provide different ways of learning, and offer opportunities for social interaction to develop higher-order thinking and understanding. The six C's—collaborating, conversing, continuing, choosing, charting, and composing—are strategies adapted for the information search process to engage students of all ages in inquiry (Kuhlthau, 1999b). Collaborating involves working together to test ideas and develop questions. Conversing is an important technique throughout the inquiry process for developing ideas and making connections that lead to constructing new understandings. Continuing involves knowing that learning is a process that requires time and persistence. Choosing is the strategy that gives a sense of control over the learning process by making choices of what to pursue, what to leave out, and what is enough. Charting depicts ideas in the form of an illustration or map that enables children to visualize emerging ideas and to share their visualizations with others. Composing is formulating thoughts in written language, not just to culminate a project, but as a tool for thinking throughout the inquiry process.

Other useful strategies for implementing inquiry may be drawn from subject area literature where an inquiry approach is applied. An excellent example comes from the reading comprehension literature. The stages of reading comprehension are similar to those revealed in the ISP research and described in the ISP model. The strategies to promote reading comprehension support a constructivist approach to learning and may be readily adopted for implementing inquiry-based learning. The sequence of strategies recommended for developing reading comprehension are: making connections, questioning, visualizing, making inferences, determining importance in the text, and synthesizing information (Keene and Zimmermann, 1997; Harvey and Goudvis, 2000). The teacher should begin by making connections with what the child already knows, then develop questions that "propel readers forward to make sense of the world." Then, children are led to visualize while they are reading to develop mental images, "pictures in the mind." Next, children are guided to read between the lines to infer notions from the text, make their own discoveries, and create meaning. They are then ready to determine importance in the text and to combine information with existing knowledge to form an original idea.

Learning through inquiry involves not only gathering information but also reading, reflecting, raising new questions, and exploring over an extended period of time to construct a deep understanding. These strategies for each stage in the inquiry process form the foundation of inquiry-based learning. Teachers and library media specialists need considerable competence in designing activities for inquiry to take hold across the curriculum. Caution must be taken to avoid activities that do not promote the deep processing required in learning through inquiry as well as the pitfalls of too much structure, too little guidance, and too few strategies. Misunderstandings arise when the traditional research project is equated with inquiry-based learning. The distinction between a project-centered approach and an inquiry-based approach lies in the underlying motivation and objective. Project-centered learning is driven by an extensive end product that actually can detract from the intended focus and objective of the learning. Inquiry-based learning is initiated by the quest to find out and culminates with sharing new understandings with others in the community of learners.

Inquiry-based learning is vulnerable to misunderstanding and fragile to change. As the case studies demonstrate, a program of inquiry-based learning requires support and nurture for development and sustainment. In a study of what constitutes effective implementation that compared successful programs with floundering efforts, certain inhibitors and enablers were identified (Kuhlthau, 1993). The inhibitors of successful implementation are lack of time, confusion of roles, and poorly designed assignments. While the enablers of successful implementation include sufficient time, clarification of roles, and well-designed assignments, several important additional requirements were identified. Successful programs require a mutually held constructivist view of learning as well as a team-teaching approach that fosters collaboration between the teacher and the library media specialist. A program of inquiry-based learning is less fragile and susceptible to change where there is a strong commitment to provide a constructivist experience for students and where collaboration between the teacher and the library media specialist is viewed as the way to provide that learning environment. In successful programs, the library media center is recognized as the essential component in inquiry-based learning.

Inquiry-Based Learning in the Information-Age School

The challenge for the information-age school is to educate children for living and learning in an information-rich technological world. The basic skills of reading, writing, and calculating need to be adapted to information-rich environments and applied to new technologies. Students need to develop the ability to learn from abundant information without becoming frustrated, distracted, or bored and to go beyond finding facts to create their own understanding at a deeper level. In response, many schools are adopting an inquiry approach to learning.

An inquiry approach occurs when students are motivated by engaging questions. They seek understanding from a wide variety of resources, raise their own questions as they learn more, demonstrate what they have learned in a number of different ways, and share their new understandings with other students in a community of learners. In this way, inquiry-based learning is compatible with the objectives of the information-age school to prepare students for the information society.

In summary, inquiry-based learning engages students in stimulating encounters with information and ideas. It is grounded in constructivist theory that builds on what students already know to form new understandings of the world. The inquiry process begins with engaging questions that motivate students to pursue their journey through the information search process. Six educational concepts about how children learn support and elaborate the constructivist theory of learning. They include active engagement, building on prior knowledge, developing higher-order thinking, supporting developmental stages and different ways of learning, and considering social interaction as an instrument of construction. In addition, library and information science research, particularly the work on the information search process, support constructivist theory.

Library Power has had the most influence on student learning in those schools where developing a constructivist approach to learning centered on the inquiry process. Many library media specialists and teachers changed their views of learning and teaching to incorporate the inquiry process as they worked together to involve students in using library resources. Inquiry-based learning was adopted as a way to prepare students for living and working in information-rich environments by engaging them in the process of learning from a variety of resources across the curriculum. Some basic strategies for implementing inquiry-based learning have been recommended as well as some suggestions for sustaining and supporting inquiry-based learning programs.

The following case studies reveal much about inquiry-based learning in the information-age school and offer many practical examples for implementation. They provide an opportunity to rethink theories about learning in order to formulate a philosophy for redesigning and revitalizing library media centers as agencies of learning in information-age schools.

References

Bartlett, Frederick. *Remembering: A Study of Experimental and Social Psychology.* Cambridge University Press, 1932.

Bruner, Jerome. *Acts of Meaning.* Harvard University Press, 1990.

Bruner, Jerome. *Beyond the Information Given: Studies in the Psychology of Knowing.* J. M. Arglin, ed. Norton and Co., 1973.

Dewey, John. *Democracy and Education.* MacMillan Publishing, 1944.

Dewey, John. *How We Think.* Heath and Co., 1933.

Elkind, David. *Child Development and Education: A Piagetian Perspective.* Oxford University Press, 1976.

Gardner, Howard. *Frames of Mind: Theory of Multiple Intelligence.* Basic Books, 1983.

Harste, Jerome. "Literacy as Inquiry." *Reading Teacher* 47 (1994): 518-521.

Harste, Jerome, and Daniel Callison. *Visions of Literacy.* Videotape produced by ITV and Special Projects, Indiana University, 1994.

Harvey, Stephanie, and Anne Goudvis. *Strategies that Work: Teaching Comprehension to Enhance Understanding.* Stenhouse Publishers, 2000.

Keene, Ellin, and Susan Zimmermann. *Mosaic of Thought.* Heinemann, 1997.

Kelly, George. *A Theory of Personality: The Psychology of Personal Constructs*. Norton and Co., 1963.

Kuhlthau, Carol. "Literacy and Learning for the Information Age." Chapter 1 in *Learning and Libraries in an Information Age: Principles and Practice*. Barbara Stripling, ed. Libraries Unlimited (1999b): 3-21.

Kuhlthau, Carol. *Seeking Meaning: A Process Approach to Library and Information Services*. Ablex, 1993.

Kuhlthau, Carol. "Student Learning in the Library: What Library Power Librarians Say." *School Libraries WorldWide* 5:2 (1999): 80-96.

Kuhlthau, Carol. *Teaching the Library Research Process*. Scarecrow Press, 1994.

Neumann, Fred, Walter Secada, and Gary Wehlage. *A Guide to Authentic Instruction and Assessment*. Wisconsin Center for Education Research, 1995.

Vygotsky, Lev. *Mind in Society: The Development of Higher Psychological Processes*. Harvard University Press, 1978.

Chapter 2

The Importance
of a Model

Jean Donham

A doption of a model of the research process is an important step toward inquiry-based learning. What is a model? How is it used in curriculum development? How does it facilitate process learning by students? How is the model used to teach the inquiry process? How is adoption of the model accomplished? These questions frame the description of one Library Power elementary school referred to as Kingston Elementary School.

Description of the School

Kingston Elementary School served approximately 550 students in Grades K–5. Nearly all parents of children in this school attended their parent-teacher conferences, and only ten percent of children were eligible for free or reduced lunch according to federal guidelines. Although the school housed a small self-contained program entitled "Core Knowledge," based on the work of E. D. Hirsch, the majority of the classrooms were not participants in this curriculum, but rather followed the district's curriculum guides. The school participated simultaneously in two major reform initiatives. The first was a literacy initiative aimed at improving teaching and learning in reading comprehension and writing, especially within the content areas. Extensive teacher inservice training was the heart of this initiative emphasizing reading strategies, the writing process, and reading and writing in content area. In the staff development program for the literacy initiative, strategies included co-teaching and model teaching by the trainers, as well as workshops and peer coaching. Through these experiences in co-teaching and peer coaching, the teachers and the library media specialist developed confidence and comfort teaching in the presence of other teachers. This comfort level seemed to be a key to facilitating collaboration between the library media specialist and the teachers. The library media specialist was a full participant in the literacy inservice activities. Through her participation, she had gained stature as a colleague among the teachers. Summarizing how teachers perceived the library media specialist, one teacher described her as "more than a library media specialist—she is a teacher with a special classroom." This initiative created a collaborative school culture conducive to collaboration between the library media specialist and teachers.

Concurrent with the literacy initiative was the Library Power initiative, which sought to integrate the library media program—especially the information search process—into the school curriculum. Strategies included strengthening the collection, ensuring open access to the library media center throughout the school day, staffing the library media center with a full-time professional, employing flexible scheduling for instruction, and supporting collaborative planning for teachers and library media specialists. The marriage of these two initiatives engendered the integration of reading and writing strategies into the information search process, especially in social studies, science, and reading. The staff development program, which had begun with the literacy initiative, was seamlessly merged with the Library Power activities by infusing the information search process into the literacy program.

The professional development in this school primarily occurred onsite. One staff developer was a library media specialist, and the other was an education specialist whose area of expertise was literacy. These two staff developers came into the school and worked side by side with teachers and the library media specialist—modeling, coaching, and guiding collaborative planning and teaching. Debriefing at the end of lessons was a frequent and effective strategy to strengthen the teaching skills of both the library media specialist and classroom teachers. Because they worked onsite, the staff developers were able to develop relationships with the teachers and the library media specialist and to adapt to their needs and interests. Workshops and inservice activities also were provided, including a summer course on collaboration where teachers and the library media specialist met to discuss how they would integrate reading comprehension instruction and the research process.

Staff development efforts were comprehensive. The focus of that work was developing collaborative relationships between the teachers and the library media specialist. When asked what had changed in the school since the introduction of Library Power, teachers at the school consistently reported that they worked more closely with the library media specialist and their students saw the library media center as an extension of the classroom. To accomplish this, staff developers met in planning sessions with teachers and library media specialists; they modeled collaborative teaching with the library media specialist and teachers, and they coached. The dynamic of this intervention was particularly noteworthy; because the staff developer was an "outsider," the library media specialist was more easily aligned with the teachers. It seems likely that this dynamic facilitated the bonding between library media specialist and teachers that was reflected in teachers' comments about how their relationship with the library media specialist had changed. As one teacher stated, "Cooperating with Nadine has made a difference. She is like a teacher as well as a library media specialist, so we work together, and skills are tied to classroom lessons."

Staff development was accomplished in a variety of formats. A "Library Lab" was held where educators from other schools observed collaborative activities in the school. During the visit, the lab was strategically planned so that observers saw a unit moving from planning to implementation. Participants in the Library Lab observed as the library media specialist and teachers taught in a laboratory situation, then debriefed with participants about the teaching decisions they had made. By providing this lab, the Kingston staff had analyzed what they were doing and had reflected on their own practice so that they were conscious of the reasons they chose to teach as they did.

On-site consultation with the library media specialist was an important aspect of the staff development activity. The staff developers met with the library media specialist to develop instructional activities that would complement the literacy efforts. They co-taught with the library media specialist to model how teachers and the library media specialist could teach together. The staff developers worked with the Kingston library media specialist to draft a chart of information literacy skills. Together they took this draft to the teachers to revise it and to identify at what grade level each information skill would be *exposed, introduced, emphasized, targeted* and *reinforced.*

Another component of the staff development effort was to encourage Kingston's professional staff members to present sessions about their activities to professional groups. Teams of teachers along with the library media specialist presented sessions for Library Power summer institutes. A group also presented a session at the conference of the American Association of School Librarians. These presentations provided opportunities for the staff to reflect on the teaching and collaborating they had been doing and to identify aspects of their work that were successful.

Collaboration is inherently more work than working autonomously. To sustain it requires affirmation and commitment. Commitment and collaboration resulted from sharing the Kingston experiences with other audiences. Preparation for these presentations caused reflection, discussion, and affirmation of their work.

Learning to work collaboratively was a primary effort at Kingston as the staff worked to integrate the literacy and Library Power initiatives. The literacy initiative included a goal of improving students' skills at reading for information. This goal engendered a disposition toward inquiry. While the topics of the school's curriculum were generated from the district curriculum, the approach to the content was the teacher's decision. At Kingston, the teachers chose an inquiry-based approach. Each unit in science and social studies began with background building followed by question generation, research, presentation of findings, and often discussion of unanswered questions. This framework cultivated the integration of information search strategies. An important finding in the Kingston case was how a model of the information search process could be used as a tool to integrate information literacy into the curriculum.

Why Adopt A Model?

Models are a part of many aspects of life. Architects present models to clients to communicate their vision for a new structure. Scientists use models to represent systems or concepts, such as the galaxy or an atom. Models are used in science and technology to track processes, such as the flow of blood or the earth's rotation. These models increase understanding of objects or systems that cannot be readily observed.

In education, models can serve similar functions. They can help to

- analyze and break down a process so we can design lessons to teach it;
- provide a common lexicon for communication among library media specialists, teachers, and students;
- guide students in the research process; and
- help us monitor what we teach and what students learn.

At Kingston School, the adoption and internalization of a model was a critical aspect of the initiative toward inquiry-based learning. A model of a process must develop from analysis of that process. When one sets out to teach a young child how to tie a shoe, the obvious need is to identify steps in that process and help the child learn the process step by step. While inquiry is not a linear process like tying a shoe, still it is a process with definitive stages. These stages have been researched and are clearly described in the literature. Foremost among researchers who have analyzed and defined the steps in the process is Carol Collier Kuhlthau, whose model is the foundation for various other models described in the professional literature and developed by individual schools and districts. Kuhlthau (1988) defines the crucial tasks in the process:

- *Initiation*: Posing questions
- *Selection*: Discussing or considering possible topics for investigation
- *Exploration*: Reading to become informed about the broad topic
- *Formulation*: Forming a focus for the investigation
- *Collection*: Seeking information to support the investigation
- *Presentation*: Synthesizing the findings into a cohesive whole
- *Assessment*: Identifying the problems and successes of the process

Conscious consideration of these stages allows the teacher to consider and teach toward the skills or knowledge the student must have at each stage.

For example, at the *Collection* stage, necessary skills include locating sources of information, accessing information within sources, understanding information in various formats, and taking and organizing notes. Teaching the process of inquiry requires analyzing the tasks that comprise the overall process and determining how to teach students to perform each of those tasks as well as how the tasks relate to one another. In short, analyzing the tasks associated with inquiry answers the question, "What do I need to teach?"

Kuhlthau's *Information Search Process Model* includes not only this cognitive aspect of the search process but also the affective aspect of information searching. Her research-based model is summarized in Figure 2-1 below.

Tasks	Initiation	Selection	Exploration	Formulation	Collection	Presentation	Assessment
Thoughts (Cognitive)	Ambiguity			Specificity →			
Feelings	Anxiety Uncertainty	Optimism	Confusion Frustration Doubt	Clarity Interest	Confidence		Satisfaction Relief Disappointment
Actions (Physical)	Seeking relevant information		Seeking pertinent information →				

Adapted from Carol C. Kuhlthau, Seeking Meaning, Ablex, 1993.

FIGURE 2-1

A Model as a Currricular Scaffold

The information search process model provided content and structure for instruction in the library media program—a scaffold upon which to organize instruction. The inquiry process itself was an important topic of instruction at Kingston— not an assumption, but an intended learning outcome. Reliance on the information search process model reminded the library media specialist and the teacher that constructs for each stage of the process needed to be taught explicitly. For example, lessons needed to be designed focusing on how to pose questions; organizers needed to be designed and provided to students to encourage continuous inquiry. Referring to the model kept these concerns forefront as lessons were prepared and instructional materials created.

Kuhlthau and other theorists generally agree that the inquiry process is not linear; instead, one proceeds along a path that may include returning more than once to an earlier stage to redirect or refine one's inquiry (Pappas and Tepe, 2001). It is common for a researcher to begin with a set of research questions and then find new questions to be posed after gaining more background on the topic. This is an important construct for students to have as part of their mental model of the information search process.

This non-linearity of the information search process was a point of emphasis with second graders early in a unit in which they were researching insects. The teacher and the library media specialist team-taught a lesson for students on posing research questions. Modeling, think-aloud strategies, and coaching were common techniques for teaching inquiry. They began with modeling questioning for a topic of their own, the praying mantis; together they generated questions about the praying mantis with the class. They began by posing two of their own questions:

> Library media specialist: One thing that intrigued me was how the praying mantis got its name.
>
> Teacher: I was wondering what it eats.
>
> Library media specialist: I wonder if it eats in a special way.
>
> Soon students were raising hands to offer additions to the list of questions.
>
> Where does it live?
>
> Does it live alone or with other praying mantises?
>
> Does it use camouflage?
>
> Is it dangerous or harmful? To whom?

Next they demonstrated how exploration into the topic might cause them to add research questions:

> Library media specialist: Let me read to you about the praying mantis. "Insects that live by killing other insects: One of the best-known hunters is the praying mantis." What question does that make you think of? I am wondering if it has anything special that makes it a really good hunter? I had not thought of that question until I started reading.
>
> Teacher: When we go to the library tomorrow, as you come across information, you may then have questions that you never even thought of.

In a second-grade class, a similar approach was taken as a teacher and the library media specialist discussed the beginning of a unit. Again, the teacher and library media specialist made explicit the steps of the inquiry process:

> Teacher: What is our goal today?
>
> Student: To choose three insects we would like to research. We are exploring today.
>
> Teacher: What is our next step after exploring?
>
> Student: Asking questions.
>
> Library media specialist: On the tables are books about lots of insects. What you will do today is browse these books and find some insects that you would like to research.

For the rest of the class session, students wrote at least three questions that could start their inquiry about insects. The next day in the library media center, the library media specialist encouraged them to add to their list of questions as they began to read. She emphasized that as they began to gather information about their topic, they were likely to return to their questioning stage to add more questions—the more you learn the more you want to know. In this way, she emphasized that they would not be done asking questions once they began reading and exploring.

The inquiry process model provided a scaffold for instructional units in this school. Units typically began with background building. The general topic of study would be introduced. Students would share what they already knew about the subject, or the teacher would provide some background. Various methods and media were used for background building. There might be a field trip to a museum or zoo to introduce the topic; sometimes a video was shown, or the teacher or library media specialist might read a book to the class. In one case, as the class was preparing to study the Holocaust, the library media specialist read several short books to the class and discussed them, beginning to raise questions about what more they might need to know to understand this part of history.

Students met with the library media specialist in small groups to read *The Lily Cupboard: A Story of the Holocaust* by Shulamith Levey Oppenheim. Students read a couple of pages, round robin, and then the library media specialist posed a question. Snapshots of the conversation reveal the engagement in inquiry. At first the library media specialist posed the questions.

Library media specialist: What does the title mean?

Student: A special cupboard.

Library media specialist: What is interesting in the picture?

Student: A broken fence so the cows could escape.

Library media specialist: What does Holocaust mean?

Student: It is about Jews and what happened to them during World War II.

Later, as the reading progressed, students moved into an inquiring mode as well.

Student: The Germans killed many Jews. That was mean. Why did they?

Student: Was this at the same time as Schindler's list?

Student: I read *The Diary of Anne Frank*, and in the house where she was hiding, there was a bookshelf that had a door behind it.

Student: They are sending their daughter away so she will be safe. Do they eventually get back to their parents of origin?

Library media specialist: I am just wondering how I would feel.

Student: Why are they wearing shoes that look like bananas?

Student: Because they are Dutch. They are in Holland.

Student: What if they take her parents or her parents die?

Student: Why doesn't her whole family stay with this family?

Student: She has got to be feeling scared.

Student: If the Germans came and wrecked my town, I would be really angry.

Student: If she takes that rabbit, it will probably jump around or make some noise, and the soldiers will find her.

Student: What does this have to do with World War II?

In the language of Kuhlthau's model of the information search process, these students were engaged in the *Initiation, Selection, Exploration,* and later *Formulation* stages of the process. (Kuhlthau, 1991)

In another class, fifth graders began their marine life research. The library media specialist asked, "Look at these photos. What kinds of things are you curious about as you look here?" Then students browsed magazine articles, focusing on pictures, charts and maps, as well as text, to begin to see what questions they might like to investigate further.

Students were encouraged to ask themselves questions as they read. They used a note-taking form (see Figure 2-2) that called for them to record in three columns: *Facts* (factual information gleaned from the reading), *Questions* (questions suggested by the narrative), and *Responses* (affective reactions to events in the reading). The three-column form had clearly structured the students' approach to their reading so that they

Facts	Questions	Responses
Her baby sister has the scours.	Will they get ship-wrecked?	She must have felt scared.
The main beam on the ship cracked.	Will people get terrible diseases?	
A new baby called Oceanus was born during a gale.	Will the food and water go bad?	
One man was swept overboard.		
Mem's family moved because they didn't want their children to learn Dutch and they wanted to get away from King John of England.		

FIGURE 2-2

focused on facts, questions, and responses to the text. The *Questions* column created a constant reminder to students to maintain a disposition of inquiry. The *Responses* column caused students to pause and reflect on their reading. When students move from this *Exploration* stage of the process to developing a focused topic, the *Questions* and *Responses* columns help them formulate the focus for their study. Such techniques for engendering an inquiring attitude toward learning were common at Kingston. Moreover, the inquiry process was content for the lessons. Figure 2-2 on page 20 shows the three-column format used as a fourth-grade class read about travel on the Mayflower.

In each unit, students were guided to formulate questions to consider about the topic; younger children referred to these as their "I wonders...," and older children called them their research questions. These questions would become increasingly focused so that they could begin to investigate a refined topic and collect information about it. Units culminated in some form of presentation of information, and finally some assessment. The unit plan framework reflected the information search process model.

A Model as an Affective Gauge

Inquiry is a process that brings with it various feelings—apprehension, excitement, frustration, worry, enthusiasm. Kuhlthau's research (1991) reveals patterns in the feelings that students have as they proceed through the information search process. Kuhlthau's model, then, can serve as a gauge for how students might be expected to feel at various stages. Adoption of a model helps everyone—teachers, students, and library media specialist—acknowledge the feelings accompanying various stages of the process and support students through those stages. At Kingston, the affective aspect of inquiry was not ignored. In the early stages of the process, both teachers and library media specialist engaged children in activities to help then formulate a topic. They read trade books to students or engaged small groups in common readings to expose children to possible topics. Sharing these reading experiences together provided opportunities for encouraging inquiry among children. This support helped students succeed through the anxiety that tends to accompany this early stage of the process when they are deciding what to study. When students engaged in Collection of information, the library media specialist encouraged students to help one another. An atmosphere of collegiality and cooperation characterized the Collection stage in the library and strengthened students' confidence and sense of direction. A model of the process that recognizes the cognitive and affective concerns helps teachers and library media specialists understand the support students need. For the students, there is comfort in knowing the early feelings of uncertainty, confusion, and doubt are normal and will yield to clarity and confidence.

A Model as a Common Lexicon

Sharing a common language among teachers, students, and the library media specialist is crucial for two reasons:

- Consistency in language of the classroom and language of the library enables children to internalize the model.

- Collaboration between teachers and the library media specialist requires use of a common language.

At Kingston Elementary School, frequent and consistent reference to the total inquiry process unpinned all teaching about inquiry. All instruction was aimed at children seeing the part-whole relationship between the lesson at hand—question-asking or note-taking techniques—and the overall research process. The school had adopted a model of the research process, an interpretation of Kuhlthau's definition of the process. The school's inquiry model was posted in each classroom and in the library. Reference to the stages in the process was frequent, and the language used to describe the process was consistent among all classrooms. The school district had developed language to describe the research process. At Kingston, the district model had been translated into child-friendly language. (See Figure 2-3.)

District Model	Child-Friendly Language
Select and define the topic	What do you want to study about <curriculum topic>?
Write and categorize known information	What do you already know?
Gather, evaluate and select materials	Let's read and find out.
Understand materials	What does that mean?
Select and record information	Let's write it down.
Organize notes	Does it make sense?
Prepare and present	Let's put it all together. Let's share what we have learned.

FIGURE 2-3

Posters of the child-friendly version of the model hung in classrooms throughout the school. These were not mere decoration—teachers referred to the posters frequently in their discussion of research activities within the context of a unit topic. In order to collaborate meaningfully, both classroom teacher and library media specialist shared an understanding of the inquiry process. Using a model for the process provided common language and common instructional goals.

Parallel teaching can be mistaken for collaborative teaching. In parallel teaching, the library media specialist may teach skills, processes, or content relevant to what is occurring in the classroom. For example, when a class is studying the Westward Movement, the library media specialist might read stories about the Westward Movement or teach students about the location of information about American history. While this is a step in the direction of integrating the library media program and the classroom, it is still some distance from true collaboration. Using an information search process model as a common lexicon, the library media specialist and teacher can approach truer integration of information process and content instruction beyond parallel teaching.

Adopting an information process model allowed both teachers and the library media specialist to own the language of the process. The library media specialist and the teacher could trade roles as expert and questioner as they helped students learn. During a lesson, the teacher might ask the library media specialist, "Where would you go for quick facts?" so that the library media specialist could then begin to brainstorm with students. Another time, the library media specialist might ask the teacher for advice on how to write an interesting lead, so that the teacher could provide the instructional input. They role-played collaboration as they co-taught. The information search process model was the common language that allowed the teacher and library media specialist to be equal participants in the teaching.

Teachers met with the library media specialist to plan lessons together. While these were often "catch as catch can" meetings, important decisions were made about what to teach and who would be responsible for each concept. Planning sessions ended with assigning tasks. For example, at the end of planning for the second grade Arctic animal research, the library media specialist had a to-do list that included co-teaching a lesson in which they would model asking questions, and another lesson on reading for information using a note sheet/log. At an informal planning session, the library media specialist and a second grade teacher met after a new research unit on insects had been started with the class. The library media specialist had determined that these students needed to learn how to use an index, and she wanted to discuss with the teacher how to fit that into the sequence. When the class left for physical education class, the library media specialist and the teacher made their plans for the next few days. The conversation began with the teacher asking for clarification on what students would do the next day. As they discussed that, the library media specialist posed the idea of an index lesson and explained why that would be useful. The teacher readily agreed, and together they planned the sequence for the next three days deciding who would take the lead for each day. Arrangements and content were set by the time the class returned from physical education class. Shared understanding of the inquiry process model facilitated communication between the teacher and library media specialist. They were speaking the same language.

A Model as a Guide for Students

In inquiry-based learning, a model can guide students so that they employ a rational and analytical approach to research. Too often, students engage in "research," but they skip important steps in the process because they lack an internalized model of the process. This tendency was described at length in the research of Judy Pitts (1996). When this happens, students define research as a process of finding an answer to a question, often someone else's question, and transferring that answer to the teacher. At Kingston, most often, the students generated research questions. The teachers wanted high quality in the questions students posed. In planning a second-grade Arctic animal project, conversation at the grade level team meeting focused on student-generated questions.

> "Will kids have good questions? How will we make sure the kids have good questions? How will we keep track of the ones they're asking?" *Teacher*

> "First we will work with them to ask questions…." *Library media specialist*

> "When they are writing their questions and their notes, they could have one page for each—food, habitat, behavior…." *Teacher*

> "We will have to see if their questions help them make the habitat and lead them to find out and write about their behaviors…." *Teacher*

Conferences with students revealed the ways in which students had internalized the inquiry process model and used it as a guide to assessing their own work. In this second-grade class studying animal habitats in science, one child described what he had done to learn about an animal and its habitat. His description closely paralleled Kuhlthau's model of the inquiry process. As background building, the unit had begun with a visit to a zoo where children observed the elements of each zoo exhibit and how the needs of each animal were accommodated in the design of its respective living environment. The students were then given the problem of developing a zoo exhibit for an arctic animal. They would need to identify facts that would be essential for designing an appropriate habitat and then find those answers. The teacher did not tell them what facts to gather— determining what they needed to know was part of their problem. At the end of the unit, Marc described his process; his description is aligned with Kuhlthau's stages. (See Figure 2-4.)

While children may not label the stages, the meaning of the process had been attained. This description of the research process parallels the information search process model adopted by the school district and translated into child-friendly language at Kingston. Internalization of the inquiry process model provided Marc and his classmates with a guide to the process they would undertake to solve their problem.

Marc's Description	Kuhlthau's Stages
"We went to the library and looked up animals, and we had to choose three. Then we wrote first, second, third choices."	Initiation
"Then we went to the library and we wrote 'I wonders' about our animal, like 'I wonder how much water it needs.... I wonder what the water temperature needs to be.'"	Selection
"Before we did our research we looked for things that would help us out, like the computer, and we found books and an animal encyclopedia. Sometimes I used the table of contents to find information in my book."	Exploration
"We had to focus our questions on facts, habitat, food, and description. So we wrote questions about each of those. Next you figure out about the animal."	Formulation
After you have a book, you just look up research. You have to look for the certain page you need, like for 'habitat.' If you look up that word you can find information. We write down the information on paper. Our paper said, 'I wonder' and then it said 'What I found out.'"	Collection
"Then we write it out on other pieces of paper in sentences to go with our dioramas."	Presentation
Marc's conference in which he described what he had done served an assessment purpose.	Assessment

FIGURE 2-4

One outcome of student-generated inquiry is excitement about what they are learning—sustained curiosity. A fourth-grade social studies class investigated life on the Mayflower and early colonial life through journal reading. During the class, lively discussion ensued as they discussed beliefs of the colonists. One girl read that "the Pilgrims believed that a person should take no more than four baths per year, because your skin might not retain the disease-killers that live there." Others commented on the use of leeches in medicine and the practice of blood letting. Students left the room at the end of the day still talking about what they had been discovering; one boy commented to his friend, "I never thought of soap as a luxury!"

End products varied. Sometimes they were multimedia productions, written reports, artistic products, or oral presentations. Students were challenged to create end products that were authentic representations of what they had learned—not simple reporting facts gathered. In a fourth grade unit about colonial life, children read widely about life in the colonies and then assumed an identity and wrote diaries to share what they had observed about colonial life. An excerpt from one journal reveals the authenticity of their learning.

The Journal of Kyra Whittle

September 14, 1627

I am so worried. My best friend, Sarah Everest, is ill. Ma won't even let me go and see her. With my chores, I hardly have any time to think of her.

Kyra

September 16, 1627

When I woke this morning, I knew that something was terribly wrong. Before breaking the fast, I asked many questions. My ma hushed me and harshly replied that Miss Everest has cholera. I cannot write more.

Kyra

September 16, 1627

Something has gone terribly wrong. The meal was much too silent. I will tell you about it tomorrow.

Kyra

September 17, 1627

I have found out that Sarah died this morning. I have not now a friend in the world.

Kyra

September 18, 1627

Today is the Lord's Day. I put on my fresh dress and Ma brushed my hair with 100 strokes and plaited it in a braid. She wound her own hair in a lady-like bun and did Anna's hair in one as well—for she is thirteen. We were on our way to the meetinghouse when we smelled smoke. It was coming from the Merriman's house. Pa left and Ma busied herself hushing the baby. And Anna was calling on the neighbors. Nobody noticed as I silently snuck away. I fetched a pail of water and brought it to Pa. At first he scolded me, but when he saw the pail he softened and forgot about me. I watched in awe as the men put out the fire. Mistress Merriman was standing by sobbing. Finally we got to the meetinghouse. The sermons were dull as usual.

Kyra

September 19, 1627

Today I am writing hurriedly because Ma and Pa have a surprise for me. Oh, I cannot wait.

Kyra

September 19, 1627

My surprise was wonderful—a new rag doll. Ma told me to go right to bed, but I had to tell you. Good night.

Kyra

September 20, 1627

This morning it snowed. Ma woke us early to help Pa clear the snow. Anna keeps hushing me. She says I must obey her for she is thirteen, and I am only eight.

Kyra

September 21, 1627

I feel very stiff. Ma made me put on my extra petticoat and cloak to help Pa with the chores. At least our home is warm. Right now we are thanking God for everything. Ma is calling me.

Kyra

September 23, 1627

I am dreadfully sorry. I have not had time to write, and I am exhausted. We are leaving Plymouth Plantation to move on to a better life at Jamestown. Sometimes I am glad that Sarah died, but only so that I do not have to say goodbye. For me, a new town will be hard. I am going to do my best. I do not think that life could get any better than 'tis now.

Kyra

By capturing the day-to-day thoughts and events of a young girl's life, this student had constructed personal meaning in her study of colonial life.

A Model for Monitoring

Student performance at Kingston was assessed by evaluating their knowledge of content and the products generated from their research as well as by determining how effectively they had engaged in the inquiry process. End-of-unit conferences were one way of monitoring the inquiry process. In a second-grade classroom, for example, the teacher and library media specialist shared responsibility for conferences with each child at the end of one unit. Each child was asked the same questions:

Tell me about your project.

How did you find your information?

Did you ever get stuck?

What was the best part of this project?

What did you learn?

Then, the teacher and library media specialist compared the findings and used the results to guide them in subsequent units. These conferences revealed not only *what* the children had learned but also *how* they had learned. In assessing students' responses, both the teacher and the library media specialist considered which tasks in the information search process model caused difficulty for students and noted what they would need to emphasize in their next research efforts.

The staff development program at Kingston was an important aspect for monitoring progress. The two staff trainers worked with the library media specialist and the teachers, coaching them in collaborative strategies, and serving as "outsiders" during reflection at the end of units. The trainers modeled collaborative teaching, performing sometimes in the role of the library media specialist and sometimes in the role of the teacher. They met with teachers and the library media specialist for planning, and they facilitated debriefing sessions after lessons had been taught. The debriefing was particularly important; during those informal, yet important, conversations, questions included, "What worked? What didn't work? What do children still need to know?"

Another way in which the inquiry process model assisted in monitoring student progress was in the development of a matrix mapping the teaching of inquiry strategies. The principal arranged for a day of meetings between the library media specialist and grade-level representatives. He hired roving substitutes who provided each team leader with two hours of substitute time; team leaders then met in pairs with the library media specialist to review a matrix indicating units taught in each grade level by discipline as well as inquiry lessons integrated into those units. While the matrix only indicated the topics of the units, it did provide an entry point for integrating information literacy into the units. This matrix provided a basis for the conversation. An excerpt of the matrix in Figure 2-5 shows the type of information included.

In each meeting, all unit topics in the grade level were examined. A primary question posed was, "What aspect of inquiry are we teaching during this unit?" The intent of this comprehensive review was to lead toward better articulation across grade levels, inclusion of aspects of the inquiry process across disciplines, assurance that all aspects of inquiry were being addressed, and an assessment of redundancy. Another issue confronted during these sessions was the need to mix large-scale and small-scale research activities so that teachers, students, and the library media specialist would not "burn out" in the implementation of their inquiry-driven curriculum. Some teachers and the library media specialist had expressed concern that too many large-scale research projects could overwhelm them, so this articulation process provided an opportunity to create balance. The inquiry process model provided a framework for monitoring student progress, for improving instruction, and for assessing the effectiveness of the inquiry curriculum.

Lessons Learned

Inquiry was central to the teaching and learning process at Kingston. There are several lessons to be learned from Kingston.

- *Adoption of an inquiry process model* was key. Consistent use of the model by teachers, the library media specialist, and the students resulted in students internalizing the process and recognizing all stages of the process. The model served as a framework for curriculum, as a lexicon

Grade Level Sample Topics: Grades 4 and 5

	Grade 4	Grade 5
Language Arts Skills	Composing: sentence structure, topic sentences, supporting details, editing, spelling Genre-related writing: letters, expository, personal narrative Oral presentation Poetry: elements, metaphor, simile Dictionary: prefix, suffix, root words	Composing: sentence structure, topic sentences, supporting details, editing, revision Genre-related writing: mysteries, expository, historical fiction Oral presentation Poetry: elements, metaphor, simile Dictionary: prefix, suffix, root words
Reading	Animals Native American tales Colonial historical fiction Author studies: Fritz, Wilder, Dahl Poetry Realistic fiction	Biography (relevant to social studies topics) Classical mythology Legends Themes: conflict and survival Historical fiction: World Wars I and II
Social Studies	Explorers Colonial history Citizenship/ Electoral process Native America	Constitution Civil War Westward movement Immigration World Wars I and II
Science	Chemistry: "mystery powders" Scientific process Electricity and magnets Life Cycles: brine shrimp Weather	Oceanography: *Voyage of the Mimi* Daytime astronomy "Kitchen physics" Levers and pulleys Colored solutions
Research	Organizers: notecards, grids, webs Expository writing Oral presentations Reading for information	Accessing information from a variety of sources Notetaking from videos and books Organizing notes Paraphrasing Bibliography

FIGURE 2-5

for communication, as a guide for students, and as a guide for monitoring progress.

- *The collaborative culture* of the school was another crucial factor. Staff development in the school had helped teachers and the library media specialist progress in efforts to work collaboratively. By modeling co-teaching and by leading debriefing sessions, the staff trainers had consciously developed the collaborative skills of teachers and the library media specialist.

- *Development of an articulated curriculum* helped to centralize the inquiry process in the educational framework of the school. Annual review of progress on teaching inquiry techniques and strategies by teachers and the library media specialist together promised continued refinement of the effort to focus attention on process learning.

- *Principal support* assisted in the implementation and continuation of efforts toward inquiry-based learning. By supporting staff development and collaboration between the library media specialist and teachers with release time, the principal facilitated implementation. This principal was not supporting only with words; he was using resources to realize the goal of an inquiry-driven school.

References

Kuhlthau, Carol Collier. "Developing a model of the library search process: Cognitive and affective aspects." *RQ* (Winter 1988): 232-42.

Kuhlthau, Carol C. "Inside the search process: Information seeking from the user's perspective." *Journal of the American Society for Information Science* 42(5) (1991): 361-371.

Kuhlthau, Carol C. *Seeking Meaning.* Ablex, 1993.

Pappas, Marjorie and Ann Tepe. *Pathways to Knowledge: The Model.* Follett Software Company. January 3, 2001.
< www.pathwaysmodel.com/the-model>

Pitts, Judy M., Joy H. McGregor, and Barbara Stripling, eds. "Mental Models of Information: The 1993–94 AASL/Highsmith Research Award Study." *School Library Media Quarterly.* 23(3) (Spring 1996): 177–84.

Chapter 3

Teacher Transformation

Dianne Oberg

U nderpinning the transformation of student learning through inquiry-based learning approaches is teacher transformation. Teachers and library media specialists have to develop personal understanding of the constructivist theory that underpins inquiry-based learning. For many library media specialists and teachers, this means more than learning about a new learning strategy; it means transforming their deeply held beliefs and well-honed practices.

In the first chapter, constructivist theory was explored as a way to understand how children learn, but constructivist theory also explains how adults learn. Teacher transformation means teacher learning. If teachers and library media specialists are going to transform their conventional and traditional teaching and learning beliefs and practices, they must have opportunities for learning. Communities of learning where students experience inquiry-based learning cannot be created without teachers and library media specialists developing new ways of thought and practice. Just as students must construct new understandings, so too must teachers and library media specialists construct new understandings. The opportunities for teachers and library media specialists to construct their own understandings, and thus to transform their beliefs and practices, may come in many different forms: reflection on practice, professional development, staff development, or collaboration.

The foundation of teacher transformation is constructivist theory. The beliefs and practices of teachers and library media specialists are transformed through active engagement and reflection on experience, through building on what they already know, and through social interaction. Teachers and library media specialists have individual personal ways of learning. They can benefit from guidance at critical points, and their learning proceeds in a sequence of stages. Constructivist theory is a broad theory about knowledge and learning that draws on work in philosophy, anthropology, and cognitive psychology (Brooks & Brooks, 1999). It offers an explanation of the nature of knowledge and of how all humans, whatever their ages or cultures, learn. It maintains that knowledge is temporary, developmental, and socially and culturally mediated and that learning occurs when individuals construct their own new understandings through the interaction of what they already know and believe with the new ideas in which they come into contact. Learning is a sense-making or meaning-making process; learning activities designed according to constructivist theory are characterized by active engagement, inquiry, problem solving, and collaboration with others (Abdal-Haqq, 1998).

Constructivist theory is not a teaching theory, but it does challenge many conventional and traditional teaching practices. Those of us who attempt to create constructivist classrooms face many troubling challenges (Windschitl, 1999). Some of these challenges include changes in teacher and student roles, changes in our images of teaching (e.g., dispensing knowledge or nurturing independent thinkers), and changes in our beliefs about what constitutes knowledge. Those who attempt to create constructivist schools or to reform schools through constructivist methodologies, face the same troubling challenges. Wagner (1998) points out the limitations of top-down school reform approaches that parallel those of traditional transmission teaching. He calls for a new practice in school change that is "consistent with our understanding of how learning takes place and how organizations change" (512). Thus, constructivist theory has important implications for school change as well as for teacher transformation.

These implications are reflected in the story of Pineview Elementary School and its journey towards inquiry-based learning. Along the way, it became clear that the changes in student learning could only occur if the library media specialist and the teachers transformed their beliefs and practices. The ways in which that transformation was supported and facilitated in Pineview Elementary School offer suggestions and guidance for others involved in trying to infuse inquiry-based learning into their schools.

Description of the School

Pineview Elementary School was located in a suburb of a mid-sized city in the southern part of the United States. The students were primarily from working-class families that lived in the area around the school. About 95 percent of the school's 530 students were African American, and about 60 percent received free or reduced-price meals. In addition to the regular K-5 classroom programs, Pineview Elementary School had some special programs: one class for Severely Emotionally Disturbed students, two for

Special Education students, and one for preschool children with developmental delays. Teacher planning and preparation time at the third- to fifth-grade level was provided through the music program with three part-time itinerant teachers and through the science program with one full-time teacher released from her previous fourth-grade assignment. It was provided at the K-1 level through the Write to Read program, planned by the teachers but monitored by a paraprofessional. Additional services to the teachers and students in Pineview Elementary School included a gifted program (a pullout program for eight students), a part-time counselor, and a part-time social worker. The school faculty included the principal and assistant principal, 22 regular classroom teachers, three special education classroom teachers, a full-time library media specialist, and several part-time itinerant teachers for speech, music, and guidance.

The school had opened in 1959, and the original building was still in use. The school was carefully maintained and decorated to give a home-like appearance; the halls, offices, and classrooms had touches of country-style décor. Displays of student work were prominent in every hallway.

The library media center was located near the main entrance and the main office of the school. The school's country décor carried through into the library media center. There were plants, small figurines, and stuffed animals everywhere. The furniture in the library media center had been used to divide the room into functional areas. The largest area, which held the majority of the reference and nonfiction materials, had oak tables and chairs for 32 students. A large cloth Mother Goose flew over this area. At the entrance to the library media center, there was a red Radio Flyer wagon, which was used for book returns. The other half of the main room was divided into a story reading area with a large comfortable couch and armchair. A row of computer stations divided the story-time area from the reference area. There was a computer and videodisc unit next to the circulation desk for teacher and student use. The library media center was an attractive and welcoming space.

Through the Library Power initiative, the school developed a relevant collection of approximately 6,000 relatively current print and non-print items. The collection was developed using the data from the Library Power collection mapping exercise, from curriculum mapping, and from the evolving nature of library-based instructional units. An analysis done for the school's 1997 Library Power report showed that new materials have been selected to be consistent with the needs identified through those analytical activities. As a result, the library media specialist stated, "The bulk of inquiries now can be supported from our collection."

Moving Toward Inquiry-Based Learning

At the end of the 1980s, Pineview Elementary School had many older teachers on staff who were steeped in the tradition of "covering the curriculum" and following the textbook page by page. The state curriculum guides were not being used, and there was a great deal of duplication of curriculum topics. Many teachers were not teaching any science at all. They were working so hard on the 3Rs that they did not think that they had time for science. The principal summarized the ethos of the school as "the more worksheets and workbooks the better." Although teachers had been trying harder, the test scores had been going down. The school was "dead last" in the rankings of the city schools on the state achievement tests; the teachers were frustrated and demoralized, and there seemed to be nothing to lose.

Then, under the leadership of the previous and current principals, a number of reform efforts began to turn the school around. Beginning in 1988, the school participated in a district project focusing on curriculum improvement through the visual and performing arts, literature, and science. At the school level, the faculty became involved in a number of curriculum improvement initiatives. Curriculum notebooks were developed for each grade level with benchmarks and pacing guides for instruction as well as curriculum content maps. A whole language program development was implemented with the support of a two-year staff development program, carried out through a combination of professional development days and monthly faculty meetings. Hands-on science became the major thrust of the science program, with students from grades 2-5 working in the science lab for two 45-minute periods every week in addition to classroom science study. These reform efforts began to develop the faculty's capacity for change and growth.

In the 1993-94 school year, Pineview Elementary School became a Library Power school. As a result of the Library Power initiative, the school refurbished the library media center, implemented flexible scheduling, extended hours, developed the collection to support curriculum alignment and pleasure reading, and engaged in various kinds of staff development. A more open attitude to the library media center as a place for many kinds of learning was reflected in an emphasis on students borrowing what they wanted, when they wanted, "within reason," and on students returning materials when they were finished using them. Flexible scheduling and open access to the library media center for individual borrowing resulted in increased student use of the collection, both for voluntary free reading and for curriculum-based activities. Students were using multiple resources for classroom-based and library-based learning activities, planned by their teacher and the library media specialist working collaboratively. The teachers and the library media specialist were working to implement a constructivist approach to inquiry learning.

The school's efforts to improve student learning have paid off in many ways, including improved performance on the state testing program. In 1995 and 1996, Pineview Elementary School was the only elementary school in the city to score above the national average in mathematics, reading, language arts, social studies, and science.

There was qualitative evidence as well that the children in the school had benefited from the constructivist approach to inquiry learning. Analysis of students' work and observations of students in the library media center and classroom showed gains in student learning where teachers were using a model-based inquiry learning approach. The teachers and the library media specialist had guided these students through the process of developing questions, locating information to answer their questions, and then sharing with their classmates what they had learned. These students, even those in the first and second grade, were able to tell or write short reports in their own words. In other classrooms, where the traditional research project, with its emphasis on product rather than process, was the norm, students were less likely to be able to tell or write reports in their own words.

Teacher Learning: Transformation of Beliefs and Practices

"Library Power was a godsend; it was the push that we needed," stated the principal. However, the changes required by Library Power could not have been implemented without teacher transformation—major changes in the way teachers thought about teaching and learning. Library Power required structural changes, such as flexible scheduling, full-time library media staff, and collaborative planning, but inquiry-based learning requires normative changes, that is, changes in the way school staffs think about the nature of learning and the kind of teaching needed to support learning. Teacher transformation comes about through normative thinking, through an interplay of inquiry, reflection, and practice. Engaging in normative thinking is much more difficult than engaging in structural thinking. "Normative thinking requires staffs to reflect critically about their schools as highly professional workplaces where teachers, students, and principals form thoughtful caring relationships" (Keedy & Achilles, 1997, 107).

Many school-restructuring efforts have failed because structural thinking (e.g., deciding to implement collaborative planning) was confused with normative thinking (e.g., re-conceptualizing how the relationships between teachers, library media specialists, and students could be supported through collaborative planning). How ironic that some proponents of inquiry-based learning believe that teacher practice can be changed through *telling*. Just as students are unlikely to become inquirers, critical thinkers, and problem-solvers through teacher telling, so too are staffs unlikely to change their traditions of *telling* as a result of the *telling* of the principal, consultant, or professional developer. This lesson can be drawn from hundreds of studies of failed implementation of laudable innovations. (See, for example, McCarthy and Peterson's 1991 study of training teachers to implement "whole language instruction.")

Teacher transformation, or changing the norms of teaching, comes about through staffs working together to critically examine (inquiry-reflection-practice) their work in order to determine "(1) why they want to change; (2) what they want to achieve; and (3) how to go about the change process" (Keedy & Achilles, 1997, 116). This requires work that has the characteristics of constructivist learning: active engagement, inquiry, problem solving, and collaboration.

Three stories of teacher learning in Pineview Elementary School reveal the nature of teacher transformation. Not all individuals experienced the transformation in the same way or at the same pace. They, like the Library Power library media specialists, changed their views of what constitutes a meaningful learning experience for students—in Year 1, a positive change in attitude; in Year 2, competence in information skills; and in Year 3, utilization of information for learning. By Year 3, many, but not all, teachers in Pineview were implementing an inquiry approach to learning in the library media center. The stories of teacher transformation give snapshots of teachers along their individual teaching journeys, moving along the continuum of understanding inquiry-based learning, from improved attitudes toward learning, to improved information skills, to using information for learning. The stories show the interplay of inquiry-reflection-practice as the teachers work with their colleagues and their students.

Stories of Teacher Transformation

The Library Media Specialist

The library media specialist had been at Pineview Elementary School for 17 years. During her first decade at Pineview, she had developed a scheduled program in library skills and literature appreciation. The highly structured program consisted of reading stories to the students and teaching skills in isolation from the classroom curriculum. The library media center was not open before or after school, and students came once a week to work with the library media specialist—an arrangement that gave teachers a break from the students and extra time for planning and preparation.

When the district supervisor began to encourage the integration of library skills instruction consistent with the *Information Power* guidelines, the library media specialist was resistant. She could not see how she could work with 22 teachers, and she had thrown *Information Power* across the room and laughed while saying, "Never in my lifetime!" At the time there was a fair amount of debate within the district over direct instruction. Then she read the work of Nancy Polette and others who advocated a whole-language approach. This experience brought her to a personal watershed. At that point, a transformation began in her beliefs about library media programming. She re-read *Information Power* and began to see how working in the ways outlined in the document could improve student learning. She shared *Information Power* with her principal, and asked for the principal's support in changing the library media program of the school. Just as the changes were being implemented, the principal was moved to a district office position. The library media specialist was unsure how the new principal would react to the changes being implemented in the library media program, but she gave the new principal both *Information Power* and a whole-language-based text by Regie Routman, *Invitations: Changing as Teachers and Learners K-12.* She asked for and was given the new principal's support to go to the faculty with the changes in the scheduling (from fixed to partially flexible) and nature of the library media program (from isolated from the classroom curriculum to integrated with the classroom curriculum). She began to work with a few teachers in the school who were interested in bringing these changes into the library media center and into the classrooms.

The Library Power initiative supported and extended the changes in the library media program and also enhanced the library media specialist's leadership role in the school. She welcomed the principal's mandate for all teachers to collaborate with her to plan instruction. In collaboration with the principal, she analyzed the impact of the library media program on student learning, comparing library media center use data with data from the state testing program. This analysis showed that as class library media center use increased so did class scores on the testing program.

The library media specialist was involved in the use of the Triple R research strategy (research, report, review) in Grades 1-3, and she could see how the teachers' use of an inquiry model helped students learn and understand their own learning processes. She realized that developing an inquiry model that could be used in Grades 4-5 might be one way to help teachers work more effectively in inquiry-based learning approaches. She began working with a library media specialist from another Library Power school on an inquiry-based model called "Steps into Research." The model would be presented and refined at a workshop for faculty at the beginning of the next school year.

The library media specialist's views of what was an effective library media program had changed dramatically, from library skills in isolation to inquiry-based learning. This transformation had involved inquiry, reflection, and practice in collaboration with her principals, teachers in her school, other library media specialists, and the consultants and researchers involved in the Library Power initiative.

The First-Grade Teacher

The first grade teacher had been teaching at Pineview Elementary School for many years, and she was about five years from retirement when the school became involved in Library Power. The principal selected her for the Library Power committee because "she was someone who was beginning to branch out from the textbook." This first-grade teacher was a thoughtful and innovative teacher. She developed and named the Triple R strategy that she used with the students almost every week (and others have emulated the strategy in the primary grades in the school). She believed that children needed to get the idea of research early in their school life and that children needed to understand that they learn from and can teach others. *The First Grade Bird Study* (Appendix C) illustrates inquiry-based learning using the Triple R strategy.

Before Library Power, the first-grade teacher had begun to use a literature-based approach, but she had not used a thematic approach to organize her teaching because she couldn't see how organizing one's curriculum around a topic such as "bears," for example, could be done in a meaningful way. At the beginning of the Library Power initiative, a question from the Library Power director at a district inservice session led her to think about the first-grade curriculum in a new way. The question was "Have you ever thought of organizing your curriculum by concepts?" As an example, the director used the concept of "change" to organize a unit of study. Looking back on this, she reflected, "I want to leave some influence on my children that will go with them for life, and I had always stressed the idea of responsibility, that they depend on others and that others depend on them." From there, she came to the major theme of interdependence. That summer, she rewrote her classroom program, incorporating its major topics into the concept of "interdependence."

I depend on others and others depend on me. (Social Studies/School Rules)

People in the community depend on each other. (Social Studies/Community Helpers)

Things in nature depend on each other. (Science/Environment)

Countries depend on each other. (Social Studies/Economics)

We depend on the past. (Social Studies/History)

The future depends on us. (Science/Ecology)

The written work posted outside the classroom demonstrated how much the individual "voices" of students were respected in this classroom. There were no cookie-cutter products. For example, after reading Pat Hutchins book, *My Best Friend*, each of the children wrote sentences about a friend their own age and then about the principal, their "grownup friend." The edited pieces, carefully re-copied for the hallway display, clearly showed the unique ideas and language of each child. The first-grade teacher was already using a model of inquiry-based learning at the time of the Library Power initiative. Her transformation related to the organization of curriculum around an important concept.

The first-grade teacher realized the interplay between structural changes and normative changes. She commented that the changes required by Library Power "were deeper than the things, the materials. They were changes in teaching philosophy, but those changes in teaching could not be changed without the materials for implementation." She stated that "Library Power brought a totally different view of the library, and it caused teaching in the school to open up."

The Second-Grade Teacher

The second-grade teacher was in her eighth year of teaching, her third at Pineview Elementary School. She team-taught with another second-grade teacher, and they worked with the library media specialist to incorporate the Triple R strategy into their curriculum. Often the units that the two teachers and the library media specialist planned together integrated the social studies and science curricula. The second-grade teacher reported that using a variety of resources made learning more interesting for the children. She stated that it was important to expose every child to the library media center and the research process. The library media center had to be more than a place to check out books.

The second-grade teacher saw a number of benefits to using the Triple R strategy. The children really enjoyed inquiry, and they also remembered things longer. Research allowed the children to go more in-depth on a topic, to ask questions, and to find out why. She noted that students, even without being asked to do so, were looking for patterns in what they were learning. *The Second-Grade Tiger Study* (Appendix C) illustrates inquiry-based learning using the Triple R strategy.

The second-grade teacher used the Triple R strategy to encourage children to explore a topic and choose what they were to learn. She and her teaching partner often started an inquiry-based learning project by asking the children what they wanted to learn. She said that the Triple R strategy placed "the children in charge of their own learning and they enjoyed that. They have input into what they and other children learn. They love playing teacher, and they are demanding of other children. They learn the information better, and the other children do too."

The second-grade teacher reported that collaborating with another teacher and the library media specialist had helped her move from using textbooks, basal readers, and worksheets. Collaboration was helping the second-grade teacher begin the transformation into a constructivist teacher, but the transformation was not yet complete. She reported that sometimes the other second-grade teacher "smacks my hand" in response to her desire to use a worksheet or reader rather than a hands-on activity or a children's picture book.

Facilitating Teacher Transformation

How can opportunities for teacher learning be created and enhanced? What roles can teachers, principals, and library media specialists play in creating communities of learning where teachers (including principals and library media specialists) and their students experience inquiry-based learning? The following five themes emerged from the case study of the implementation of Library Power at Pineview Elementary School.

Faculty Capacity for Change

For Pineview Elementary School, the implementation of the structural and normative changes involved in the Library Power initiative required an ameliorative change rather than a radical change. The successful implementation of a number of reform efforts, beginning more than five years before the school became a Library Power site, had developed the faculty's capacity for change and growth. Library Power was a catalyst for inquiry-based learning, and there was consistency of purpose and approach among inquiry-based learning and a number of initiatives that had been started earlier. For example, whole-language and inquiry-based learning both emphasize the use of a wide range of trade books and other literary and informational materials; curriculum alignment and inquiry-based learning require collaboration among teachers and the library media specialist; hands-on science and inquiry-based learning emphasize exploration and problem-solving. Inquiry-based learning was not seen as a radical change by the faculty of Pineview Elementary School, and, in fact, some of the faculty saw it simply as an enhancement of the school's practice.

Instructional Leadership of the Principal

The principal at Pineview Elementary School had a clear view of her role as instructional leader in the school, and she used administrative routines to reinforce best practices in teaching. She reviewed teachers' yearly plans and required them to hand in daily lesson plans every other week. She checked to make sure that the displays of student work were instruction-oriented. She reviewed the minutes from each of the grade-level planning meetings. She provided performance data to teachers for their classes, and she expected teachers to adapt their teaching on the basis of that information. She and the assistant principal visited classrooms on a regular basis. The principal incorporated support for Library Power activities into her instructional leadership role in the same way. From the beginning, she made it clear to her staff that participation in the Library Power initiatives was mandatory. For example, she required each teacher to document and present evidence on an annual basis of having planned with the library media specialist three times a year. Teachers who failed to do so received reminder letters reiterating the expectations for collaborative planning with the library media specialist. The principal provided attention to inquiry-based learning and the library media program; she visited the library media center; she discussed the library media specialist's plans, and she reviewed data on use and circulation of materials.

Shared Leadership within the School

The principal, the library media specialist, a teacher, and a parent developed the Library Power proposal. In most matters related to Library Power, the principal and library media specialist worked as a team, consulting with the assistant principal, taking major issues to the school's Curriculum Committee, and putting together ad hoc working groups for specific tasks, such as writing grant applications. About 25 percent of the classroom teachers at Pineview Elementary School were playing a leadership role in the implementation of Library Power: working with the library media specialist and other teachers to develop minigrant applications and modeling collaborative planning in their work with the library media specialist. Some of the teacher leaders were also chairs of their grade-level planning teams. The principal assigned teachers within the school to ensure that there was a strong curriculum leader in each grade-level group. In hiring new staff, she and the vice-principal were looking for teachers who would plan and share with other faculty. This approach was a continuation of the principal's commitment to having teachers who would be able to undertake the instructional work needed to continue to improve student learning.

Collaboration

Flexible scheduling allowed teachers to plan library-based activities in blocks of time, and it allowed them to use the library media center in response to student's questions—at the teachable moment. All faculty members responsible for a homeroom were engaged in some level of planning with the library media specialist by virtue of the school-wide expectation for grade-level planning. Although collaboration with the library media specialist was mandated, some teachers met this requirement minimally. About 25 percent of classroom teachers worked in partnership with the library media specialist, planning formally and instructing together. About 50 percent worked with the library media specialist to some extent, planning informally and getting occasional assistance with some aspect of resource location or instruction. Another 25 percent had little interaction with the library media specialist; for those teachers, opportunities to learn with and from each other were limited. The library media specialist participated in grade-level meetings and also planned individually with teachers. The mini-grant system adopted by the local public education foundation also provided an incentive for teachers to work with the library media specialist; classroom materials and supplies as well as library materials could be obtained through the mini-grants. The minigrant program required collaboration, and this was used by the library media specialist to encourage collaborative planning of library-based activities at grade levels where this kind of planning had rarely been done.

Teacher Learning

Pineview Elementary School had been involved in a variety of staff development activities prior to Library Power. These included the faculty's work on whole language and curriculum alignment. The principal was committed to student-centered learning. She mandated teacher inservice training for the 1992-93 school year based on Regie Routman's *Invitations: Changing as Teachers and Learners, K-12*; teachers were assigned chapters to read and discuss at faculty meetings. The purpose of the Library Power Committee, according to the teacher member, was "not so much to lead as to share information, to get the idea and then to get started in educating our people." At the beginning of the school's involvement with Library Power, the library media specialist and one other teacher went to a one-day collection mapping workshop and a week-long Trainer of Trainers workshop on collaborative planning. These were sponsored by Library Power. The library media specialist and various members of the faculty participated in the workshop sessions provided by the Library Power director. The library media specialist and faculty particularly noted the sessions on essential questions, collaboration, and leadership. Another kind of professional development for the library media specialist, sponsored by Library Power, was the visit to another Library Power school.

A number of faculty members mentioned that the process of writing local Library Power mini-grants was an important professional development activity, and this idea was supported by an analysis of the mini-grant applications. The applications required a unit plan or other description of instructional activity. Some of the first applications included a lot of reproducibles; the later ones showed movement to student involvement in evaluation, portfolio assessment, and expectations of student reflection on the learning process. The collaborative work of developing mini-grant applications was changing teachers' views of what constitutes good teaching practice, and it also increased the commitment of the teachers to the instructional activities that were funded by the mini-grants. This finding is consistent with Showers and Joyce's work (1966) on the power of collaboration being at least equal to peer-coaching for the effective institutionalization of instructional innovations. Figure 3-1 summarizes how staff training strategies influence transformation.

Pineview Elementary School also has been providing professional development for others. In the summer of 1996, the principal, the library media specialist, and a teacher, along with a library media specialist from another Library Power school, provided a three-day workshop for district principals, teachers, and library media specialists. On three occasions, these four, working as partners, also have provided workshops for area principals and library media specialists. On more than 12 occasions, Pineview Elementary School hosted teams of visitors from other schools. Teaching others through these activities enhanced the professional growth of these leaders from Pineview. Staff development activities maintained the momentum after the Library Power initiative was formally over. A workshop for faculty on the research process was being planned for the following autumn. At that workshop, the library media specialist would introduce an information search process model called *Steps into Research,*

Staff Development Training Components

Component	Influence
Presentation of theory and rationale	Up to 10%
Presentation of theory and rationale PLUS Multiple modeling or demonstration	10% to 30%
Presentation of theory and rationale PLUS Multiple modeling or demonstration PLUS Practice with feedback	80% to 90%
Presentation of theory and rationale PLUS Multiple modeling or demonstration PLUS Collaboration with observation (no verbal feedback)	80% to 90%

Based on the work of Bruce Joyce and Beverly Showers, beginning in 1980.

FIGURE 3-1

a local adaptation of the classic information search process model developed by the library media specialist and a library media specialist from another Library Power school.

Conclusion

A major change like the switch to inquiry-based learning cannot readily occur without teacher transformation. Teacher transformation at Pineview Elementary School was far from universal; teachers varied in the extent to which they changed their beliefs and practices in line with a constructivist approach. At the time of the case study research in Pineview School, all teachers appeared to believe that inquiry-based learning improved students' attitudes toward learning. Some teachers supported inquiry-based learning because they believed that it would improve students' information skills. A smaller number of teachers, about one-third of the faculty, had a good understanding of inquiry-based learning as a constructivist approach to helping students use information for learning.

In Pineview Elementary School there was evidence of changes in teachers' practices and beliefs. The commitment to the changes brought by involvement in Library Power was reflected in a statement made by at least four different faculty members: "The kids won't let us go back!" Other comments included:

The integrated approach will not disappear. There has been a change of attitude in our children. They feel that they have the power, and the teacher is there to help them. These children are not afraid to learn. (5th Grade Teacher)

Library Power has had a real impact on children's learning. It has shown students what they can do. They are not so quick to say, 'I don't know.' They are willing to find the answer. They take more pride in their learning when they have some input into their own learning. (Assistant Principal)

I hope that we continue and keep growing. I am afraid some schools will lose this. It has been taken up so well here. Many teachers have seen how it is successful and have liked it. We feel the library is open to us. We are less tied to the textbook and more willing to take a chance, to develop new approaches. (3rd Grade Teacher)

The Library Power changes are deeper than the things, the materials, although they were certainly a boost and encouragement, and the changes could not be implemented without the materials. Library Power supported a change in the philosophy of teaching. It brought a totally different view of the library, and it caused teaching here to open up. It feels like you came from 'seeing darkly' to a space full of light. We won't lose that. (1st Grade Teacher)

Teacher transformation in Pineview School was facilitated by the faculty's history of successful change; the visionary leadership of the principal; the sharing of leadership roles among the principal, the library media specialist, and the teachers; the opportunities for teachers to work together; and the opportunities for teachers to learn together. One of the educators at Pineview School expressed these ideas this way:

"[The previous principal] had been leading us toward a literature-based integrated curriculum. This started the ball rolling. [The library media specialist] was pushing us in this direction too. When Library Power came, we were ready for it. We have had strong academic leadership from two principals and from the library media specialist, who was very motivated and very strong-willed. One by one, teachers began to like the changes. Initially, faculty members were directed, but they became participants. When you plan your own curriculum, it's going to go better. This is a hardworking faculty. We get along well, sharing and cooperating. Here we all just push it down each other's throats!"

To develop inquiry-based learning in most schools requires more than structural changes; it requires transformation of both beliefs and practices related to learning and teaching. The development of inquiry-based learning at Pineview school was led by the principal, the library media specialist, and a core group of teachers who held student-centered, constructivist views of learning and who had personally transformed their practice in ways consistent with inquiry-based learning. The faculty's confidence in making changes in the school's program had grown out of a history of successful collaboration and curriculum innovation. The development of inquiry-based learning approaches at Pineview Elementary School, facilitated by the Library Power initiative, contributed to improvements in student achievement in measurable ways and holds promise for continued improvements in student learning.

Lessons Learned

- *Faculty capacity for change:* A faculty that has experienced successful instructional innovation, such as curriculum alignment or hands-on science, will be able to do the transformative work required for an instructional innovation, such as inquiry-based learning. A faculty that has experienced failed innovation will need greater support, time, and encouragement to be able to address an instructional innovation such as inquiry-based learning; the faculty also will appreciate an honest acknowledgement and analysis of the errors made in the failed innovation attempt.

- *Instructional leadership of the principal:* A dynamic and forceful principal, focused on student learning and curriculum change and knowledgeable about the school district and community, can build support for inquiry-based learning in the school and community. A principal can use routine administrative structures to emphasize teachers' use of the library media center, to encourage collaboration among the teachers and library media specialist, and to reinforce student-centered teacher practices.

- *Shared leadership within the school*: The teamwork of the principal and library media specialist can enable an instructional innovation, such as inquiry-based learning, to be implemented in a powerful way. The leadership of classroom teachers, as well as that of the principal and the library media specialist, is important in implementing an instructional innovation, such as inquiry-based learning:

- *Collaboration*: Schools where people share their ideas and where there are structures in place to facilitate teachers' working together are more able to implement an instructional innovation, such as inquiry-based learning. Flexible scheduling provides the opportunity for teachers to use the library media center in a more integrated way and to work together to develop a deeper understanding of inquiry-based learning.

- *Teacher learning*: Staff development is critical for the implementation of an instructional innovation, such as inquiry-based learning. Staff development is more powerful if it is part of the instructional practice of the school. Staff members will progress in their learning at individual rates and in personal ways. There is no one-size-fits-all staff development.

References

Abdal-Haqq, I. *Constructivism in teacher education: Considerations for those who would like theory to practice.* Washington, DC: ERIC Clearinghouse on Teaching and Teacher Education, 1998. ERIC Digest ED426986.

American Association of School Librarians and Association for Educational Communication and Technology. *Information Power: Building Partnerships for Learning.* Chicago: American Library Association, 1998.

Brooks, J. B., & K. G. Brooks. *In Search of Understanding: The Case for Constructivist Classrooms.* 2nd ed. Alexandria, VA: Association for Supervision and Curriculum Development, 1999.

Keedy, J. L., & C. M. Achilles. "The need for school-constructed theories in practice in US school restructuring." *Journal of Educational Administration,* 35(2) (1997): 102-121.

McCarthey, S. J., & Peterson, P. L. (1991). *Reflections on restructuring at Lakeview School: Views of teachers and their literacy practice.* Paper presented at the Annual Meeting of the American Educational Research Association, Chicago, IL.

Newmann, F. M., H. M. Marks, & A. Gamoran. "Authentic pedagogy: Standards that boost student performance." *Issues in Restructuring Schools, Center on Organization and Restructuring of Schools,* University of Wisconsin-Madison, 1995, Issue Report No. 8.

Routman, R. *Invitations: Changing as Teachers and Learners, K-12.* Irwin, 1991.

Showers, B., & B. Joyce. "The evolution of peer coaching." *Educational Leadership.* 53 (6) (1996): 12-16.

Wagner, Tony. "Change as collaborative inquiry: a 'constructivist' methodology for reinventing schools." *Phi Delta Kappan,* 79(7) (1998): 512-517.

Windschitl, M. "The challenges of sustaining a constructivist classroom culture." *Phi Delta Kappan,* 80(10) (1999): 751-755.

Chapter 4

Resources: Facilities, the Collection, and Personnel

Kay Bishop

F acilitating inquiry-based learning demands access to information resources that are relevant to the topics being explored. The mix of people and resources necessary to implement inquiry-based learning is fragile. The breadth and depth of available resources must increase to accommodate students' individual needs. Likewise, the physical facility must accommodate the increased use of the school media center by multiple groups throughout the school day.

How is collection development different in an inquiry-based learning program? How do the facilities affect inquiry-based learning? How is collaboration among the school library media specialist and teachers implemented using student-generated inquiry? These questions will be addressed in the following case study of a middle school that was part of the study of the impact of Library Power on student learning.

Description of the School

Corbett Middle School was going through numerous changes during the implementation of the Library Power initiative and the evaluative case study. One professional school library media specialist, an A-V paraprofessional, and a media clerk served the media needs of 1,098 middle-school students in Grades 7-9. The ethnic background was primarily Caucasian. Only 74 students at the school received free or reduced-fee lunches. The majority of students came from the well-kept, middle-class homes that surrounded the two-block campus of Corbett Middle School. The school had a fairly large special education program. Students with disabilities were mainstreamed into the regular classes during part of the day, and gifted students could participate in special classes in English, math, science, and social studies.

The school, which had been built in 1963 for 650 students, was suffering from overcrowding. Classes met in the halls; the cafeteria served as a physical education classroom; and students practiced their musical instruments on the stage of the auditorium that was too small to be used for all-school assemblies. At noon, the salad bar and snack lunch lines spilled out into the large hall in front of the school office. Relief from the overcrowding came the following school year when two new middle schools opened. Total student enrollment in Corbett Middle School dropped to 820, and the school lost several of its faculty members to the new middle schools.

Inquiry-Based Learning at Corbett Middle School

Before the implementation of Library Power at Corbett Middle School, there were no major educational reforms to introduce inquiry-based learning into the curriculum. However, an active Library Power committee at the school directed the activities of the Library Power initiative, including implementing projects that emphasized student inquiry. The heaviest users of the media center and its resources at Corbett Middle School were the seventh and eighth grades, which were divided into middle-school teams, while the ninth grade functioned as the standard first year of high school. Inquiry-based activities were collaboratively planned and discussed in the seventh- and eighth-grade team meetings each week. The dynamic library media specialist was actively involved in the team planning of these projects and took part in the after-school professional development activities funded by Library Power grants.

To integrate library skills into the inquiry-based research projects, the library media specialist chose to use materials from the district guide to information literacy. The guide was written to "provide strategies for mastering the skills needed for information literacy," with the central purpose being "to enable learners to become effective in locating, interpreting, evaluating and communicating information." The guide included several lesson plans, some based on Michael Eisenberg and Robert Berkowitz's *Information Problem Solving: The Big Six Skills Approach to Library & Information Skills Instruction* (1990). It also provided lists of literacy skills and suggested research topics for various grade levels. The library media specialist at Corbett Middle School stated that she regularly collaborated with teachers who incorporated the components of the guide into their assignments and evaluations.

One inquiry-based unit, "Celebrating Differences," was created at a summer workshop. The seventh-grade teaching team that planned and implemented the interdisciplinary unit had made a commitment to the ideal that all children would be successful in the classroom, including the students with special needs. To achieve this goal, the unit centered on accepting individual differences.

In the seventh-grade English class, the students considered the differences among the characters in the movie *Star Wars*. Students were asked to look around their classroom and see how they differed from one another. They analyzed various axioms, such as "Beauty is only skin deep" and "You can't tell a book by its cover." To help them look at what is acceptable in different cultures, students viewed *The Eye of the Beholder*, a movie from the *Twilight Zone* television series. The students also analyzed and compared different learning styles, using a Lotto-type Bingo game. The assignments in the unit were constructive in nature. Students participated in role-playing handicapping conditions and wrote bio-poems about themselves. In one activity, the teacher asked, "If you were going to design a page for the World Wide Web, what would it look like?" The students responded by making a collage about themselves on pizza disks. Discussions and role-plays were designed to guide the students to in-depth understanding of differences among students. Students were encouraged to be actively engaged in reflective thinking, a characteristic of inquiry-based learning.

The social studies team member participated in the unit by having his students research various cultures. He met with the library media specialist to plan the four days that the students would spend in the library media center gathering information on cultures in the United States and throughout the world. Before coming to the media center, the students filled out the first two columns of a form entitled, "What I Know, What I Want to Learn, and What I Have Learned." Later, after referring to resources in the media center, some of the students wrote brief comments in the form's third column, "What I Have Learned." These steps of inquiry are similar to those discussed by Kuhlthau in the beginning paragraph of Chapter 1.

The library media specialist's method of preparing the students to gather information centered on some critical-thinking skills and questions. "If you had to pack your suitcase and move to your culture, what would you want to know?" she asked. "How cold is it there? What clothes do I need to take? What will we eat?" The library media specialist then suggested that the students write their questions. The library media specialist also asked the students, "Who is going to evaluate your project? . . .Yes, your teacher will, but before you give it to your teacher, you'll evaluate it. You'll know whether you've done a good job, and you'll know what you have learned." Both the library media specialist and the social studies teacher introduced some excellent media resources that would be helpful to the students. The library media specialist encouraged the students to use the best resources they could locate while the teacher talked to the students about not simply photocopying pages, but trying to select from the resources that would be most helpful in answering their questions. The students were told that during the first day of research they would not be allowed to use the electronic resources in the media center. "The Library Power committee and other teachers have selected some excellent resources on cultures to add to our collection, and I want the students to take advantage of the wonderful print resources we have," the social studies teacher explained to the researcher. He added, "Many of the students have multimedia encyclopedias on computers at home, or they will come back at lunch time or after school to get information from the computers." The library media specialist ended the introduction to the resources by stating, "Begin your investigation!"

Several students used handouts provided by the library media specialist to assist them in gathering and organizing their data while other students devised their own organizational methods for gathering and organizing their data. The flexibility to encourage students to use their own strategies, while offering assistance to students who needed it, shows the intent of the school to help students become independent in the information-search process.

During this unit of study, the researcher observed three students. They did not exhibit the feelings of uncertainty, optimism, and confusion that accompany the first three stages of Kuhlthau's research process. These students spent little or no time in the early stages of the information search process; their task was well determined by the assignment, so the anxiety and uncertainty that often accompanies these early stages was absent. They seemed to start experiencing the fourth-stage feeling of clarity, and then moved from there through the fifth-stage feeling of direction, and finally to the sixth-stage feeling of satisfaction or dissatisfaction. In all three cases, the students expressed satisfaction in the final stage.

In analyzing the research processes of the students, one could say that in their class activities their teacher and the library media specialist most likely moved the students through the first three stages of Kuhlthau's model: initiation, selection, and exploration. The students did not begin to work independently until the fourth stage (focus formulation), which coincides with the feelings of clarity.

One might also speculate whether the collaborative preparations and careful guidance of the social studies teacher and the library media specialist might have lessened the feelings of uncertainty in the first stage and confusion, frustration, and doubt in the third stage of Kuhlthau's ISP. In fact, Kuhlthau (1989) has noted some of the problems that have surfaced in her studies dealing with the research process: insufficient time for students to work through the process under the guidance of librarians and teachers, a lack of planning time for team teaching among librarians and teachers, and the lack of a teaming of librarians and teachers in which both parties are aware of their responsibilities in the research assignments. None of these problems seemed to be present in the culture project. On the contrary, the seventh-grade classes researching cultures were given sufficient time in the library media center under the guidance of both the teacher and the media specialist. The teacher and the library media specialist cooperatively planned the research and were cognizant of each person's responsibilities. In some instances, such as helping the students identify and locate appropriate resources, the responsibilities were shared with no apparent difficulties.

All the students working on the culture project submitted a written paper with a bibliography of at least three references. In addition, students were given options on how they could construct and present their information to their classmates. Shari, who chose to present her information in an attractive yellow construction paper travel brochure, made the following comment to the researcher:

> I learned a lot from this project. I didn't know anything about Tahiti at first, except it was an island. I think it must be beautiful there, but I found out it would be expensive to travel there. I really like to learn about places. It is something you can actually use. If someone ever says anything about Tahiti, I can say, "Oh yeah, I know that."

Matthew, a mainstreamed student with a language disability, made a less sophisticated product than several of the other students, presenting his information on the sides of a Kleenex box or "culture cube." He read his information to the class and experienced difficulty in pronouncing some of the words, but when another student asked a question about his culture he was able to accurately respond. His comments about learning in this project were reflective and insightful:

> It was extremely interesting. I learned about the government and language. If I move to Venezuela or anyone asks me about it, I can tell them. I thought about it [the project] after I finished it—about how people are different from us and yet the same. It was fun, too.

Cassie's project was the most creative of the three students observed by the case study researcher. She had several items that were handmade, including elaborate colorful posters with photographs and a large interactive *Jeopardy* quiz board that she had designed, using the information that she had found about Tanzania. Cassie, who attended some gifted classes, was very confident in her presentation, and the students were extremely attentive. She used no notes but simply told her classmates about some of the things she had found particularly interesting about Tanzania, such as the very young boys herding cows and the presence of tsetse flies that cause sleeping sickness. The teacher encouraged Cassie to play the

Jeopardy game with the students, and most of the students in the class raised their hands and wanted to answer questions.

Even though their resulting products differed in completeness and complexity, all three of these students were actively engaged in inquiry-based learning. Cassie's projects (the written paper, the *Jeopardy* game and colorful posters, and the class presentation) were the most elaborate; yet, both Shari's and Matthew's comments indicated they had experienced constructive learning that they could apply outside the school curriculum. They had even transferred the learning to possible future uses. Matthew's products were the least sophisticated, and yet his responses about learning were reflective and insightful, providing evidence of an in-depth understanding of cultural similarities and differences. The differences in the apparent abilities of these three students and the evidence that all three students experienced authentic learning in their projects demonstrate the fact that the inquiry-based process of research works well with students of all abilities.

An interdisciplinary unit on the Great Depression prepared by one of the eighth-grade teams included other inquiry-based activities. The students researched buildings and places in their own community, concentrating on what they were like during the 1930s. Students selected their own topics and presented their information in the format of a tour guide talking to an audience on a tour bus. The teacher, in fact, had arranged for an actual bus tour to occur a few weeks later. All parents and several local and state dignitaries were invited to join in the bus tour, which was scheduled to visit all the sites in and around Springfield that the students had researched. The students acted as the tour guides, using the bus microphone to present their information in an interesting manner. "Extra, extra. Read all about it. Stock market crashes," was the attention-getter used by one student to introduce the historical background of the *Springfield Star*, which had been two newspapers before they merged in 1931. One group of students researched Springfield High and began their presentation with a cheer from the 1930s. Another student munched on potato chips while she talked about her uncle, who had worked at the Weaver Potato Chip Factory. The students were especially eager to share their feelings about this inquiry-based research:

> We learned you don't have to limit yourself to books. You can call people and places and use articles. It's more interesting than anything I've done on a project.
>
> I like it here. I've lived here all my life, so just the background of it is kind of neat to learn. I think it's more fun doing it [research] with things here because you can experience it when you're here and stuff.
>
> I felt like a reporter for a newspaper. I had to go out and find all this information.

The students' responses indicated that although they had to work particularly hard to gather the information for this project, they enjoyed the research, applied it to their lives, and felt as if they would remember it better than any other research they had done. The value of this inquiry-based research went beyond the classroom setting, and the students gained and shared in-depth knowledge about many local places. Construction of meaning sometimes runs the risk of not being as creative as it might be if too much structure and direction are given to the students. In this instance, the students were given little in the way of structure, except for the importance of an attention-getter. Consequently, the students' products demonstrated much variety and creativity.

While most of the ninth-grade research at Corbett Middle School seemed to be the traditional format of researching a topic and producing a formal research paper, one ninth-grade biology teacher's approach was quite different. She collaborated with the library media specialist and a ninth-grade English teacher to plan a unit dealing with animals in different phyla. The biology teacher encouraged the students to explore an unusual animal in their phylum. Students were given the option of working individually or with a partner. Students spent several class periods in the media center finding information about the animals in both print and nonprint resources. Several students used the Internet, CD-ROM programs, laser discs, videos, and posters that were available in the media center. The librarian noted that she was able to see the students develop skills in the use of both print and electronic materials. She stated, "I saw many of the literacy skills we'd worked on earlier come to a level of understanding not seen before. Students could work independently after the initial class period. All the resources and skills finally meshed, and they were feeling success."

The students made 15-minute presentations to their classmates, using videos, video laser discs, and posters that were borrowed from the library media center. In addition, each student built a three-dimensional model of an animal, and those models, which were made from various media—a koala bear made of cotton balls and spray-painted gray; a sea anemone constructed from red and white pipe cleaners; a brown clay bear sitting on a rock; and a spiny anteater made with fur, clay, and painted toothpicks—were displayed in the media center. A third constructive product included stories written by the students. In each story, the students included at least five facts about an animal in their phylum. Sixty-three of the stories were selected and bound in an attractive green spiral book entitled *Animal Stories*. The book included titles such as "Mossella the Dugong" and "Bob the Echidna." Students delivered the books to elementary school library media centers in Springfield. Some of the students' reactions to this inquiry-based project were:

> I liked the project better than taking notes in class. It was not so structured. There were no set limits, and we didn't have to take a test on it.

I liked writing stories. I wrote about a kangaroo, and I had a chance to be creative. There were no limits set with the writing.

When we received a thank you from an elementary school that we gave the book to, it made us feel appreciated.

If I went to a zoo, I could recognize the animals, and I would know their habits and behavior.

It was really nice to do this kind of research in both classes because we had more time. They gave us time to work on it in both biology and English. We went to the media center three times in English and twice in biology.

I thought it was pretty nice we were getting a grade in both classes. It helped that we went to the media center in both classes.

This entire unit was particularly strong in constructive learning experiences based on the inquiry process. The students produced several elaborated products and were called upon to locate, organize, synthesize, and utilize information. Additionally, they created information when writing their animal stories. The students' comments indicated that they were involved in inquiry-based learning. The library media specialist noted that this was the first project in which there had been collaboration among the biology teacher, the English teacher, and herself. She was hopeful that the success of the inquiry-based research would encourage other such projects with those teachers, as well as with other ninth-grade faculty members.

These were just a few of the numerous inquiry-based activities observed by the case study researcher at Corbett Middle School. The inquiry-based learning at the school included not only classroom assignments but also activities that involved students' personal interests. The researcher observed several inquiries made by students coming to the media center individually. After expressing their questions and what they already knew about a topic, they informally researched topics such as how to start a coin collection, how to find information about Olympic Medal figure skaters, and how to improve one's basketball skills.

These examples of projects demonstrate that some of the students at Corbett Middle School were actively engaged in inquiry-based learning that would help them prepare for living and learning outside the school. The teachers and the media specialists involved in the projects planned together to provide ways for students to build on their present knowledge and to develop higher-order thinking skills and understanding. They encouraged students to converse during the inquiry process and to share information with their classmates.

As Kuhlthau pointed out in Chapter 1, an important distinction between a project-centered approach and an inquiry-based approach to a research project lies in the underlying motivation and objective. While some of the units and projects at Corbett Middle School were driven by the product—which can sometimes detract from the objective of learning—those described in this chapter were based on the quest to find information and share it with others, which is characteristic of the inquiry-based approach. The projects involved were well designed; the roles and responsibilities of the teachers and the library media specialist were clearly designated; and the students were given sufficient time to complete the inquiry process and reflect on their new understandings and learning.

At Corbett, the resources available to support inquiry-based learning were particularly important to their success. Previously, the facilities were unattractive and limited, and the collection was dated. Improvements in these resources facilitated the move toward inquiry-based learning. Personnel in the school and the library also played a key role in undertaking this initiative.

Library Media Center Facilities

Corbett Middle School's library media center was located at the far end of a ground-floor hall. The media center's high open-beamed ceiling extended to the top of the second floor, exposing a view to the second-floor computer lab, which opened onto a small balcony overhanging the circulation desk.

Before the media center was renovated with Library Power funds, a stairway led to the balcony and second-floor rooms. In the renovations, the stairway was removed, making the second-floor computer room inaccessible from the library media center. The removal of the stairway opened a large wall area and floor space, making it possible to add furniture that housed a variety of magazines and newspapers, high-interest/low-level books on audiotapes, a large picture-poster file, and a comfortable reading area. Many of these materials were purchased through the Library Power grant.

An additional renovation to the library media center was the removal of a wall that opened up a classroom area, which was then called Media West. This area was used to house a major portion of the nonfiction collection, a career file, a vertical file, eight circular tables and 32 student chairs. The addition of Media West increased the seating capacity of the media center from 60 to 89. "The renovation funds have enabled us to create two classroom spaces, thus serving more students each period," noted the media specialist. A pull-down projection screen in Media West made it possible to show videos in the room without interfering with the other classroom seating at the far end of the library media center. A bulletin board with student-produced posters and papier-mâché masks brightened the room.

Improving the lighting in the library media center also was part of the renovation plan. The existing lights cast a hazy, orange glow and many shadows. They were replaced during the second year of the case study evaluation. "I thought I'd come in here on my planning time and get a suntan," joked one teacher, while a student observed, "It seems like there are skylights in here now."

Although Library Power funds could not be used for technology, they were used to purchase much of the new furniture in the library media center, including a circular workstation, which accommodated networked Macintosh computers loaded with numerous software programs. The computers, which were in almost constant use by both students and faculty, also had Internet access. Faculty members and students frequently mentioned the changes in the renovation of the media center:

> **A special-education teacher:** It was very hard to do research in here before. The library was not very user-friendly. It was crowded, and tall shelves blocked the light from the windows. The library media specialist had the shelves cut down, letting in the window light, and she took out the metal stairs, which weren't used by students anyway.

> **A seventh-grade math teacher:** It has been great to have extra space and to be able to expand with the removal of the walls. Now we can have two classes in the media center during a class period. This has really helped double the number of students using the media center.

> **An eighth-grade student:** It is amazing how different this media center looks. I was in here many times—even before I was a student since my brother and sister went to school here. The big, long circulation desk wasn't here. And it was dark. I love to come here now. I come whenever I can.

Renovating this library media center doubled the number of teachers coming in with classes and also attracted many students who chose to come to the media center on their own. These students were observed in a variety of inquiry-based activities, many of which were related to their personal interests and questions, not just to the assignments in their classes.

The Collection

Undoubtedly, the Library Power funds given to Corbett Middle School for collection development had one of the greatest impacts on inquiry-based learning activities. Before the Library Power initiative, the collection at Corbett Middle School was outdated and was not used extensively. The materials to support research and inquiry-based activities were extremely limited. The library media specialist described the collection:

> When I came here four years ago, our collection was bad. For many years there had been no money budgeted to the media center for collection development. Our nonfiction was outdated. Most of our books were from the

1970s. More than half of our paperback collection needed to be replaced. We did not have current materials to support the sciences and social studies. Many of our nonfiction books were at a reading level too high for our students. There was a real shortage of high-interest/low-level fiction and nonfiction reading material. Materials in the vertical file were outdated. There were very few audio materials to accompany literature, and many of our audio materials were very old. We had no multimedia materials and no laser discs. And we needed periodicals that are of interest to teens.

A situation such as this one could do little to support the inquiry-based learning that was being encouraged by Library Power, research studies, and professional library literature. Consequently, the faculty at Corbett Middle School decided to use a major portion of the library funds for collection development. Being involved in Library Power also meant that the local school district was required to contribute some matching funds to improve the collection. The library media specialist at Corbett Middle School reported that Library Power offered the school the opportunity to update an old, worn-out collection of books and other print materials and use district funds to purchase core collection titles, audiovisuals, and computer software.

Outdated, unused, and stereotypical materials were weeded out of the collection. Titles in all areas were added to increase the multicultural perspectives. Seven thousand dollars of Library Power funds plus $6,000 of local funds were used to purchase nonfiction books in the 300, 400, 500, 600, and 900 areas. Serious deficiencies had existed in all these areas, and all teachers submitted wish lists, with department consultants meeting with the library media specialist and making the actual requests. In several instances, the library media specialist and teachers previewed the materials before adding them to the collection.

The reference collection also was targeted for major improvement. Sets of reference books on careers, biographies, world cultures, science, technology, and general information were purchased.

The case researcher observed large numbers of the seventh-grade students using these nonfiction and reference materials for their inquiry-based research on world cultures. The well-organized materials were attractive, age appropriate, and contained numerous illustrations that were especially appreciated by the students.

Using a combination of local and Library Power funds, the school increased the number of audio books for student checkout by 100 percent. These books were ordered in collaboration with the Special Education (SPED) students and staff. The library media center staff reported (and the researcher observed) that the SPED students became heavy users of these materials.

Outdated and worn audiovisual materials were weeded from the collection. Again using a combination of local and Library Power funding, posters, prints, kits, laser discs, and CD- ROMs were added to the collection, particularly in the areas of science and art. Teachers requested specific titles in drama, art, and English. These materials were used heavily by students to create class presentations of their inquiry-based research, such as for a ninth-grade biology unit, a Greek mythology thematic unit, and a plate tectonics project in seventh grade.

A small amount of funding also was used to add items to the professional development collection, which the library media specialist had previously reported as being underused. The library media staff, in collaboration with the faculty, increased the number of books on the Internet, middle school philosophy and practices, and adolescent psychology.

Staff and students were keenly aware of the availability of the resources and the differences the new resources made to inquiry-based research and authentic student learning.

A seventh-grade teacher: In our plate tectonics project, I wanted to make it possible for the students to use self-discovery. The students used the study prints and laser discs from the media center to make class presentations. Using the magazines on the electronic computer, they were able to get to the most recent materials. Resources for science have greatly increased and made a real difference in learning. We are able to do much more research, and the kids feel more successful because they can now find the resources they need. Before all these resources were available, many of the teachers did not use the media center much with their classes.

The Special Education Coordinator: Originally, there weren't a lot of books in the media center for the special-education students. One push that I saw with Library Power was for the talking books. We supported this push and matched the Library Power funds with SPED funds. There just weren't many materials for these students if they were going into the media center with a regular English class. The students (special education) are really happy being with the other students, and now they are feeling very positive about finding materials in the media center.

An eighth-grade teacher: When we started the Greek mythology project last year in English class, at first I wasn't too sure about it because I didn't know where all the information would be, and I thought it would be hard to find some of the pictures I needed. After I kept working on it and went to the media center where I found some other books, I felt much better. I liked the art projects that we did with it too, so it was fun to put it all together, and I felt good about it.

An eighth-grade student: There are a lot more books in the media center now. The books are newer and more attractive. It makes us want to come down here more often.

An eighth-grade English teacher: When I started at this school seven years ago, this media center was worthless. The collection was old, and we didn't have the materials needed for research. Sue [fictitious name for the media specialist] is the next best thing to God. She really pays attention to our interdisciplinary curriculum and gets us the resources we need. And that makes it a whole lot better for our students.

Teachers also used the media center materials for their own reference, and some teachers checked out materials to take to the classrooms. One of the art teachers reported that she relied heavily on library media center resources, using the center once or twice a week for her own reference to reinforce her teaching. A seventh-grade math teacher commented that he used the media center often with his students, but because it was sometimes heavily booked, he also took library media center materials to his classroom. For one assignment, he checked out a classroom set of almanacs to teach students how to identify and check the accuracy of sources. These almanacs were used in a unit in which the teacher taught the students that there is more than one way to find information, that there are multiple sources of information, and that sometimes there are conflicts among the sources.

One of the seventh-grade English teachers made extensive use of the library media center resources in her classes. She stated that she believed students should be engaged in exploring their own literature choices; thus, she had the students actively read and discuss books, maintain reading logs, and respond to the books in weekly letters. Students obtained the majority of their reading materials from the library media center. They also led the book discussion at least once, designed an individual project to show their understanding of the book, and presented the project to the class. Students also wrote process papers explaining their projects.

Several of the seventh-grade students shared with the researcher the projects they had developed for this unit and for other units in which they had used the library media center resources in their English class. The following are some of their comments:

> Reading has become a favorite pastime for me. I enjoy it much more now, and it's easier to make myself read.

> After we read the book, we wrote it as a play, and we did the play in the media center and had props and costumes. It was kind of the finale of the year.

> I have intitled [sic] this picture "The Never Ending Battle." That is the feeling that I felt was portrayed through the book *Many Waters*...The reason I call this the never ending battle is because there will always be the conflict between the good and evil on the earth. And even if the good doesn't always win, there will always be a battle between the two.

> The teacher talked about how books were made. And we wrote books— the summary, the jacket, all about the author, and a dedication.

The assignments in these classrooms that used the resources in the media center demonstrated many of the characteristics of authentic learning and disciplined inquiry. Without a wealth of relevant, current resources, the learning would not have been as meaningful or accurate.

After adding the new materials to the library media center collection, Corbett Middle School's library media specialist reported that the staff and students were becoming more aware of the resources. Teachers began to work more on interdisciplinary units using inquiry-based activities, and people were more aware that the media center is a source of all kinds of materials. She stated that there seemed to be an increased comfort level for the students and the staff.

From these examples of students and faculty members using the resources in the library media center, it is obvious that both the quantity and quality of the collection has an impact on inquiry-based learning. A large number of current, age- and ability-appropriate, attractive, interesting, and relevant materials in a variety of formats are essential for the success of inquiry-based learning. Such materials need to be selected for purchase by matching the inquiry needs of students and teachers to the most appropriate resources. Thus, the library media specialist must keep abreast of the curriculum, the interests and special needs of both teachers and students, and the availability of quality resources.

Personnel

The interactions of personnel has an impact on inquiry-based learning in a school. The fact that the media staff at Corbett Middle School worked well together—almost functioning as a family unit in their caring and respect for each other during and after school hours—contributed to a pleasant library media center atmosphere that was conducive to inquiry-based learning. The staff demonstrated excellent rapport with both the students and faculty. They welcomed all persons entering the media center, and the researcher observed a philosophy of service toward all users. The administration was supportive of the media center, its importance to the curriculum and the Library Power initiative itself. Thus, the possibility of success for collaboration to increase inquiry-based learning was high at this middle school.

Corbett Middle School's faculty members were involved in several collaborative planning and interdisciplinary teaming workshops funded by Library Power. More than 50 teachers and administrators showed their commitment to interdisciplinary teaming by attending a Library Power planning workshop after school. Along with the library media specialist and administrators, the teachers developed ideas for specific interdisciplinary units they could use in their classrooms. The participants made the following comments in written evaluations of the workshop:

A teacher: Give us some time and the freedom to try.

An administrator: This is definitely…by far…no holds barred…the best committee at Corbett Middle School! I listen to this, and it makes me wish I were back in the classroom. I think the thematic concept of teaching would be fun to try.

A teacher: Very thought provoking. Really gets you thinking about what you can do.

A teacher: I would like to know how much/or if the Library Power committee would be willing to help compensate/supply teams with materials to help develop interdisciplinary units.

These workshops greatly increased the collaborative planning among teachers and the library media staff, among faculty members in different disciplines, and among the school staff and community.

Several collaborative units were undertaken during the two-year case study. Besides those already mentioned, teachers of an eighth-grade English class and a special-education class were paired to study the Civil War. They took three field trips together, including a visit to John Brown's Cave in Nebraska City to view part of the Underground Railroad. The students in the English class kept a journal of their experiences with their special-education partners. The teachers also reported that the library specialist was very helpful, not only by purchasing the books, but also by helping the students find and use the resources in the media center. The project was successful in providing authentic learning experiences related to the Civil War. Additionally, the students gained a relevant and in-depth understanding of special-education students.

Some other collaborative activities included a study of the Renaissance period and a Renaissance Festival to which all the school staff and seventh-grade families were invited. There was also a unit in which 75 eighth-grade students participated in several activities with nursing home residents, a multicultural Asian-American unit that was fraught with elaborate art activities, four author visits, and numerous reading incentive projects.

When the researcher visited Corbett Middle School after the first year of the Library Power initiative, the library media specialist provided a folder with 21 units in which she and the teachers had collaborated. She explained that in her opinion *collaboration* is a relative term. She noted, "I would say around 50 percent of the teachers do some kind of collaboration, but for some teachers that means just coming in and telling me what they plan to do in the media center and what I can do to help them."

After participating in collaborative activities, several faculty members and administrators viewed the collaborative opportunities as having a positive influence on student inquiry-based learning:

An eighth-grade teacher: Students remember what they have heard in other disciplines and classes. There is a huge carryover of learning, and the learning is more focused, less disjointed. At first, the students were a little leery, but not anymore. They really like the interdisciplinary units.

A program facilitator for staff development: One of the most helpful things that Library Power has done is provide time for teachers to work on units. This takes much teacher time, and in addition to the time provided by Library Power, the teachers have given much of their own time.

The students also expressed opinions regarding the relevance of learning in the collaborative interdisciplinary units, as demonstrated in the following comments:

It made it easier to understand when both classes did it. In English when we read *The Reluctant God*, we would come across a vocabulary word that we had learned in social studies, and then you remember, "Oh yeah, I remember that from social studies."

It's better than the teachers just telling you all the stuff because you have to read it and present it, and you get a lot more out of it.

You have to find the information yourself, so you remember it better. You can use any resources that you can find.

It is obvious from the comments of both the faculty and students that collaboration at Corbett Middle School was having a meaningful impact on student inquiry-based learning.

Although there did not seem to be any set mechanisms to insure that collaboration took place, it was apparent that the library media specialist and other media staff members were eager to assist teachers or students wanting to use the media center services. Through memoranda and at meetings, the library media specialist invited the teachers to plan cooperatively with her. When she oriented new teachers to the media center facilities and resources, she emphasized the potential for collaborative activities. She noted that time was the biggest barrier to collaboration since everyone on the faculty was so busy.

The Impact of Changes at Corbett Middle School

During the first year of the case study, all indications were positive regarding the institutionalization of the changes influenced by Library Power and the adoption and spreading of inquiry-based learning. However, some factors in the following year had great impact.

At the end of the first year (when the two new middle schools were scheduled to open in the fall), a call went out for faculty volunteers to transfer to others schools. According to the district contract, forced moves were made by seniority; thus, some of the teachers volunteered to move to other schools, knowing that if they did not, they would not get to choose where they would be placed. Some of the teams that had worked well together requested transfers so they could remain together. Several of the teachers who left Corbett Middle School were what the media staff called "the movers and the shakers." The media secretary shared her observations: "We lost an awfully good group.

Many were the teachers with less seniority. They shared new ideas and were motivated. They helped put a spark into the media center when they came in."

The library media specialist echoed those sentiments: "The big library users and big supporters of Library Power have moved on. They were our converts who were brought into the program [Library Power principles and inquiry-based learning]. They saw how Library Power could be used and how it benefited the students." According to the media specialist, the loss of several teachers also "decimated" Corbett Middle School's Library Power committee, with only one committee member, besides the media specialist, remaining at the school.

During the second year of the study, the media secretary reported that circulation was definitely down, and the loss seemed to be somewhat high proportionally to the decrease in student enrollment and faculty members. She remarked that perhaps this was due to the loss of the teachers whose classes had been heavy users of the media center. The library media specialist noted, however, that the media center still seemed to get large numbers of drop-in students.

Although changes during this second year of the study did affect the usage of the media center, there was evidence that some of the remaining teachers were beginning to "buy in" to some of the opportunities provided by the media center and Library Power. It is also important to note that all schools in Springfield, including the high schools, were following the principles of Library Power and had received funds from Library Power or the local educational foundation to implement the principles. Thus, the "movers and shakers" who were transferred to other schools in Springfield most likely took with them the positive media center experiences that they had at Corbett Middle School. Hopefully, they became proactive forces in the use of collaboration and planning activities that would result in inquiry-based learning in their new schools.

The media staff agreed that although there were fewer classes using the media center during the second school year, they themselves were as busy as ever with the new changes in technology—installing a security system, preparing the collection for an automated circulation system and card catalog, and overseeing the student use of the Internet and the new computer software programs and CD-ROMs that had been purchased.

Another major change occurred in Corbett Middle School when the principal suffered a heart attack in late fall of the second year of the study. The assistant principal took over as interim principal until the end of the year. Although he was supportive of the media center and the media center personnel, he had not been at Corbett Middle School as long and had much less experience with the Library Power initiatives.

At the end of this second year, the media specialist, administrators, and several faculty members expressed concern about the future, noting that the faculty would once again be reduced in the following year when the large ninth-grade class would graduate and a smaller seventh-grade class would enter. The interim principal explained, "We have a 650-student projected enrollment, but 750 to 800 is really more ideal for a middle school. Next year, we won't have enrollment for two full seventh-grade teams, and some teachers will need to cross content areas and grade levels." The media specialist decided to accept a position in a high school media center the following fall. She took with her the A-V paraeducator from Corbett Middle School.

Institutionalization of educational reforms is complex. Changes in personnel radically affected inquiry-based learning initiatives at Corbett Middle School. Unlike Kingston Elementary School, described in Chapter 2, Corbett had not adopted an information-search process model, so there was no vestige of the teaching of the process left for newcomers to continue. In comparison to Pineview Elementary School, described in Chapter 3, Corbett had made strides forward in structural change, but normative changes in the teachers' beliefs and practices had not yet matured. This left the inquiry-based learning program vulnerable, and indeed, much of the progress was not sustained through the transitions in personnel.

This case study demonstrated the importance of several factors in the implementation and institutionalization of inquiry-based learning in school media centers. Attractive, well-organized, spacious facilities make it possible to increase the number of students and faculty members using the center, thus making it possible for more students to do research and participate in inquiry-based discovery. A large collection that is current and relevant to the needs of the students and teachers helps motivate and sustain inquiry-based activities. Enthusiastic, flexible personnel, who are trained in the principles of inquiry-based learning, are more apt to collaborate and provide units of study that encourage authentic, relevant student learning. Changes in any of these elements can have an impact on implementation of inquiry-based learning.

Lessons Learned

- *Faculty support for change:* When a new program (such as Library Power or inquiry-based learning) is introduced into a school, it is important to gain the support of all faculty members and administrators, or the program runs the risk of non-sustainability as staffing changes take place in the school.

- *Early intervention by the library media specialist:* Introducing students to possible resources that might help answer their questions is helpful to students who are beginning inquiry-based research.

- *Student-developed structure:* Providing too much structure for an inquiry-based activity can be inhibiting for some students. It is better to let the students create some of their own structure and organization.

- *Time for collaboration:* Providing enough collaborative planning time between the library media specialist and the teacher, delineating the responsibilities of the library media specialist and the teacher, and giving students sufficient time in the media center under the guidance of both the library media specialist and the teacher will increase the success of inquiry-based learning activities.

- *The information search process model:* Using an inquiry-based model, such as Kuhlthau's ISP, rather than an information-transmission model, will make it possible for students to experience learning that is grounded in a constructivist foundation and will help students produce understandings that have meaning and value in their lives.

- *Authenticity of learning experiences:* Inquiry-based activities are successful in producing authentic, meaningful learning for all students, regardless of the innate abilities of the students.

- *Multiple resources:* Students prefer inquiry-based research that encourages the use of many types of information formats: books, periodicals, pamphlets, posters, videos, laser discs, audiocassettes, Internet, CD-ROMs, and interviews.

- *Interdisciplinary approaches add interest:* Students enjoy interdisciplinary units that use inquiry-based activities and think learning is easier when there is carryover from one class to another.

- *Student determination of the product:* If given the opportunity, students can produce a variety of creative products that demonstrate inquiry-based learning. All students do not need to produce the same type of product for authentic, relevant learning to take place.

- *Inquiry-based learning should become natural:* Inquiry-based learning not only should be evidenced in classroom assignments but also should be encouraged and nurtured in the personal interests of students.

- *Student reflection:* Providing opportunities for students to reflect during the research process, converse with other students, and share their understandings will increase the chances of inquiry-based student learning.

- *Attractive facilities encourage students:* In order to encourage students and teachers to make full use of a school library media center, the facilities must be attractive and comfortable, provide good lighting, and be able to accommodate at least two classes, plus groups of individual drop-in students. If such conditions do not exist, the media center may go unused and will not be able to play an active, vital role in the curriculum and in inquiry-based learning.

- *Collection*: A large current, relevant collection, comprised of both print and nonprint materials that are age- and ability-appropriate, is essential if inquiry-based, authentic learning is to take place in a school library media center.

- *Participative collection development:* Collection development in a school engaged in inquiry-based learning involves input and active participation from the teachers, as well as the library media specialist. Collection development should be based on the questions and needs of the students and teachers.

- *Teacher-library media specialist collaboration:* Planning mechanisms to implement collaboration with teachers will help increase the number of teachers who actively participate in collaborative planning with the library media specialist.

References

Eisenberg, Michael, and Robert Berkowitz. *Information Problem-Solving: The Big Six Skills Approach to Library and Information Skills Instruction.* Greenwood, 1990.

Kuhlthau, Carol, "Information search process: Summary of research and implications for school library media programs." *School Library Media Quarterly.* 16 (1) (1989): 19-25.

Chapter 5

Conclusion

Jean Donham

Inquiry-based learning requires commitment to an understanding that learning is an active process—one that demands learners take ownership and responsibility for their learning. Only when students leave our schools as persons who engage in question-raising as well as answer-seeking will they indeed be lifelong learners. We hope to graduate an independent learner—one who has both the skills and disposition to engage in inquiry.

These case studies highlight important elements that support such a fundamental shift in the way curriculum and instruction work in schools. Foremost is the change in teacher practices and beliefs about learning. Whereas teachers traditionally may have been experts who presented students with questions and answers, an inquiry approach invites students to generate questions and seek answers to their questions. Whereas teachers traditionally may have taught in isolation, an inquiry approach is facilitated by collaboration with a library media specialist. Together they guide students in their quest for information and develop in students the skills and dispositions to be effective information seekers and users in response to the queries they raise. Whereas teachers traditionally may have posed questions for students and assigned them to find answers, in this approach, teachers encourage students to generate questions.

This disposition toward inquiry—sustaining the innate curiosity that young people often have—creates special demands on the resources that must be available for the unanticipated questions. Whereas information-search skills may have been assumed in the past, this emphasis on inquiry demands that students understand and have a complete mental picture of the information search process. Such a mental picture can come from consistent adoption of an information search process model in the school.

The primary lessons learned from these cases are that an inquiry approach to teaching and learning

■ engages students in construction of their own meaning rather than in transfer of information from one source to another;

■ supports deeper understanding;

■ benefits from adoption of an information search process model throughout the school to provide common language among teachers, students, and library media specialist and to help sustain focus on inquiry;

■ benefits from students having their own mental model of the information search process so that they expect of themselves the question-raising, exploring, searching, reflecting, analyzing, evaluating, synthesizing, and communicating that make up the process;

■ improves when teachers and library media specialists work together to discuss what needs to be taught, plan how it should be taught, and assess the outcomes;

■ requires access to a variety of current information resources that can meet the needs of inquiring students;

■ benefits from access to a library media center and library media specialist throughout the school day; and

■ requires a sustained effort over years with leadership and commitment to institutionalize it.

School reform often fails for lack of persistence and true institutionalization. Inquiry-based learning is as vulnerable as any school reform undertaken. It is hard work, and it demands a fundamental shift toward constructivism. The roles of teachers, library media specialists, and students change. The definition of curriculum itself is tested as we ask whether there is a finite list of facts that must be learned or whether learning to learn about a topic can, in fact, become the curriculum. These cases show that there must be a commitment to inquiry, and there must be resources—both human and physical. There must be continuous and collaborative effort to implement it, and there must be regular assessment of progress. The transformation of schools to engage children in inquiry requires a shift in normative thinking (i.e., re-conceptualizing how teachers will teach and how children will learn) as well as structural thinking (i.e., the mechanical and organizational steps of implementation).

This is no small order for today's educators. The question that remains in the forefront: Is it worth this effort? Children who are eager to learn, children who raise questions and study problems in depth, convince us that it is, indeed, worth the effort to transform schools in the direction of inquiry-based learning. We hope the lessons learned at these schools can begin the journey for other schools—schools where children can be inquisitive and be encouraged to keep asking *How?* and *Why?* and *Why not?* and *What if?* and. . . .

Methodology

Kay Bishop

Introduction

The three case studies described in this book were part of the evaluation of the Library Power initiative, which began in the fall of 1994 and continued through June 1997. Dianne McAfee Hopkins and Douglas Zweizig, professors in the School of Library and Information Studies at the University of Wisconsin-Madison, were the principal investigators of the evaluation. Norman Webb, Senior Scientist for the Wisconsin Center for Education Research, and Gary Wehlage, Professor of Curriculum and Instruction, School of Education, were also part of the central team of investigators. More than 50 researchers contributed case studies of Library Power schools or district sites for the evaluation of the Library Power initiative. Three of these case studies (those described in this book) focused on the impact of Library Power on student learning. Carol Kuhlthau, Dean of the School of Communication, Information and Library Studies, at Rutgers University, and a well-known researcher in the area of school libraries and information-seeking behavior, oversaw these case studies.

Research Methods

Some quantitative measures were used in the evaluation of Library Power, but qualitative research methods primarily were used in the three case studies that focused on the impact of Library Power on student learning. The school library media specialists at each of the three schools completed extensive questionnaires that asked for both numerical and qualitative information dealing with staffing, collaboration, facilities and equipment, scheduling, inservice training, collections, library and information skills, and student learning. Local documenters visited the schools during the two years of the case studies. The documentation they gathered was provided to the case evaluators.

The case study researcher for the middle school spent three weeks (two during the first school year and one during the second) at the school site. The two researchers for the elementary school case studies each spent two separate weeks during one school year at their sites. The case study researchers gathered and analyzed data for their research using the following methods:

- Observations made primarily in the media center, but also in classroom settings (these observations were documented with field notes)
- Semi-structured interviews with school library staff, school administrators, and faculty members (in some cases, these interviews were recorded using audiocassette tapes)
- Semi-structured focus groups of students (these groups were usually tape-recorded, using audiocassette tapes that were later transcribed)
- Numerous informal conversations with library media staff, faculty, and students
- Content analyses of school library media center documents, such as lesson plans, media center schedules, memos, and Library Power reports
- Content analyses of written reports by the Library Power documenters
- Content analyses of teachers' units of study and worksheets
- Content analyses of student-produced projects and conversations with students relating to a variety of their projects, including written reports, stories, poems, biographies, journals, photographs, posters, travel brochures, and models
- Observation and content analysis of a video containing students' classroom presentations

Not all methods of the described data collection methods were used at every school.

Assessment of Student Learning

One of the frames of reference for the assessment of the student learning process in the three schools included the criteria for judging successful student learning as defined by Newmann, Secada, and Wehlage (1995): construction of knowledge, disciplined inquiry, and value beyond school.

1. Construction of knowledge is described as the expression of knowledge in written or oral discourse, such as papers or speeches; the actual production of things, such as videos or works or art; and performances, such as musical concerts or athletic events.

2. Disciplined inquiry emphasizes the cognitive processes involved in learning. It consists of the following features: using a prior knowledge base; striving for in-depth understanding rather than superficial awareness; and expressing conclusions through elaborated or complex communication, such as narratives, justifications, or dialogue rather than in brief responses, such as answering true-or-false questions or filling in blanks.

3. Value beyond school refers to student accomplishment that has a value beyond being an indicator for success in school. The value can be utilitarian, aesthetic, or personal.

The other frame of reference used in the case studies was the seven-stage model of the information search process that has been identified in Kuhlthau's research (1993). This model was referred to while investigating the research processes of the students at the three schools. The two frames of reference are complementary and provided the case study researchers with guidance for gathering and analyzing data that related to student learning. The use of the inquiry approach was emphasized in the judgments relating to student learning.

The researchers were directed to address some general questions that had been posed by Hopkins and Zweizig, the evaluation directors. These questions included:

- Are students having different learning experiences as a result of Library Power?
- Are students engaging in more independent research?
- Are students approaching topics/subjects in new ways?
- Are students conducting high quality, independent research (i.e., are they better at locating and evaluating sources; are they better at integrating information?) and does this seem to be related to Library Power?
- Are students acquiring a broad, in-depth understanding of topics due, for example, to less reliance on sole-source instruction?
- Are students performing new tasks that may be associated with active or constructivist learning?

Analysis of Data

Research data were analyzed using a content-analysis approach. This involved a lengthy process of reading and re-reading responses, noting the content of responses, identifying categories from the responses according to the content, and then grouping and re-grouping the responses to develop themes.

Codes were assigned to the categories and themes, and those codes were placed in the margins to help organize the data for analysis and reporting. Themes included topics such as collaboration, principal support, school community, collection, facilities, disciplined inquiry, constructivism, connection between school and the "real world," multiculturalism, professional development, author visits, reading incentive programs, technology, and institutionalization. One of the case evaluators also used a highlighting technique, applying different colors to differentiate comments made by students, teachers, media personnel, and administrators.

Case study evaluators verified information by checking back with administrators, school library media specialists, and teachers. In some instances, they clarified information or added additional information. Carol Kuhlthau and Dianne McAfee Hopkins reviewed all three case studies. When necessary, Kuhlthau and Hopkins asked the case evaluators to further verify information, alter some parts of the report, or find additional information that they thought should be added to the case studies.

References

Kuhlthau, Carol C. *Seeking Meaning: A Process Approach to Library and Information Services*. Ablex, 1993.

Newmann, Fred M., Walter G. Secada, and Gary Wehlage. *A Guide to Authentic Instruction and Assessment: Vision, Standards and Scoring*. Wisconsin Center for Education Research, 1995.

Inquiry Organizers

Kay Bishop and Jean Donham

I nquiry-based learning gives students responsibility for generating
questions, designing a strategy for seeking information about the
questions, making meaning out of the information found, and communicating new learning. As students become more sophisticated in
these processes, they will create their own methods for organizing their
work. However, they often will benefit from having organizational
schemes to assist in their thinking. Two organizational schemes that
were used in the Library Power schools described here are the KWL
and the QUAD formats. (See Figures A-1 and A-2.) These two
approaches place emphasis on student-generated inquiry and offer an
open-ended approach to the information-search process. KWL represents Know—Want to Learn—Learn. The KWL technique can be
particularly helpful as students *explore* a topic, and the KWL strategy
directs them toward a focus as they learn more about it.

The QUAD can be helpful in the *Collection* stage of the information
search process. QUAD assumes a clearer definition of the topic and
guides students in organizing the information they are collecting around
the questions they generate. By providing reminders for information
about references, this format helps students prepare themselves for development of their final product, complete with citations.

KWL
*What I **Know**, What I **Want** to Learn, What I Have **Learned***

Topic_____

Before Reading	Questions	After Reading	Resources
What I already **know**	What I **want** to find out	What I have **learned**	Where I found the information

FIGURE A-1

QUAD
Questions, Answers, Details

Topic_____

Questions	Answers	Details
1.		
2.		
3.		
4.		

References		
Author	Title	Copyright Date Volume/Page
Author	Title	Copyright Date Volume/Page
Author	Title	Copyright Date Volume/Page

FIGURE A-2

Stories of Student Learning

Dianne Oberg

O bserving a classroom where children are engaged in inquiry-based learning helps the observer gain a mental picture of the process. These two scenarios describe inquiry in classrooms in one of the case-study schools. In this school, the *Research—Report—Review* strategy is used to help students move through the inquiry process.

First Grade—Bird Study—Research, Report, Review

Four first-grade researchers arrived in the library with their clipboards and their questions, ready to learn about feathers. With the guidance of the librarian and using library books and pictures she had selected, they located information and talked about the different types of feathers and how they help the birds. The librarian had a selection of feathers, which they examined and discussed, noting the different textures of the feathers, the little hooks holding the feathers together, and the hollow quills of the large feathers. They used droppers of water to test the water resistance of the different kinds of feathers. Then the students were asked to tell the most important information they had found, and the librarian recorded the facts on a small whiteboard mounted on an easel next to their table. The group then put the facts in order and copied them onto their clipboards. The Research phase of the process had been completed.

The students then returned to their classroom with their clipboards, the feathers, and the droppers. Several students had been working with their teacher using a Big Book about birds. They were divided into four "little classes." The four researchers who had worked in the library media center assumed roles as teachers and each reported what they had learned about feathers to a "little class."

The teacher then called the class together in a large group with the "authorities on feathers" seated at the front of the group. She began, "Tell me one thing that you learned about feathers today." One boy volunteered, "Fly. Feathers let birds fly." The teacher nodded and asked, "Who taught you that, Josh?" Josh replied, "Courtney taught me that.The teacher continued with this pattern around the group, until all the "students" had spoken. Then she invited the "teachers" to report on anything that had been missed in the discussion. They also performed the water resistance demonstration for the class. Next the group that had been working with the Big Book shared what they had learned, and then the whole class read the Big Book in unison. The Review phase of the process had been completed.

The Triple R strategy is a model of inquiry learning based on constructivist principles. Using this approach, children were involved in making sense of information, presenting what they had learned in their own words or drawings. They were building on prior knowledge, finding similarities and differences, and making decisions about information that would fit their need or answer their question. The children in the first grade were finding similarities and differences among kinds of feathers, choosing the information about feathers to report back to their classmates, and then presenting that information to their classmates. The bird study in first grade built on the knowledge and interest that children have about living things, and the librarian encouraged them to decide what kinds of information they wanted to find about their topics. Finding the desired information, putting it into your own words, taking notes, organizing the information, and creating a presentation format are the next tasks in the information search process. The first-grade students were expected to find information from within the resources selected by the librarian. The librarian helped them find the information about their topic. She encouraged the students to put the information into their own words and encouraged them to put the information into order.

Second Grade—Tiger Study—Research, Report, Review

The second-grade students were studying tigers as part of a unit on animals of Asia. The students came as a small group with small booklets (four-door shutter folds). The librarian was seated at a table in the reference area ready to greet them, with a globe and a small stack of books. She began with a discussion about the location of Asia. They found Asia on the globe and then began to discuss where they could find information about tigers. They decided to look in the general and animal encyclopedia under "T." As they found articles about tigers, they began to read aloud from the articles. The librarian encouraged them and asked them to find information that they wanted to share. She also read aloud from an article and asked questions to help direct the information search: "What does a tiger look like? How much do they weigh? How do they hunt?" She guided them to form sentences out loud and began to record their sentences on the whiteboard easel. When the board was full, she said, "Before we put this on paper, let's look back and see how we want to organize this."

She read the sentences and pointed out the category where the sentence might fit. Then she asked, "What is best to start with?" Kristen wanted to start with babies, but the librarian suggested they begin with a general description. When they had decided the order, with some help from the librarian, she read the sentences aloud in the new order. "Does that flow? Super job!" The students copied their information (five facts) onto one of the four pages of their shutter-fold booklet and then returned to their classroom. Over the week, the same basic pattern was followed with three more groups, with each group researching a different animal of Asia. This was the Research phase of the Triple R.

The Report phase on tigers took place in the classroom. The teacher announced, "My teachers are getting ready. Students, make sure your desk is clear of everything but your four-door shutter fold. Your job as students is to ask questions. Here are your teachers. Teachers, are you ready?" The "teachers" took turns reading their facts about tigers. Then, the "students" asked questions, which the "teachers" answered (with a little help from the classroom teacher). Next, one of the "teachers" wrote the five facts on the board, and the students copied the facts onto their shutter folds while the other "teachers" moved from desk to desk, monitoring the work. In the midst of this, one "student "asked, "Why do tigers live alone?" The teacher repeated the fact that had come from the research phase—"Lions live in groups, but tigers don't"—but did not appear to probe further. However, later that afternoon, the teacher returned to the topic to carry out the Review phase of the process. The teacher reminded the students of the question raised in the Report phase, and the students shared some of their ideas about the question. One of the students compared the tiger to the panda, an animal studied earlier, and said that the panda was not a social animal either. One of the students returned to the library to further investigate the question with the librarian, and the process continued.

Inquiry-based learning should begin with the children having or developing background knowledge of the topic. This should be done in such a way as to develop children's interest in and commitment to the topic. Once children have developed their knowledge of and interest in the broad topic, they should be involved in determining the questions they will investigate and how they might find the information they need about a particular topic selected from the broad topic area. These tasks require children to engage in "deep processing," to think about the information they have and the information they want, or to consider how to present information to a particular audience. From a constructivist viewpoint, learning also involves exploration and developing personal connections with what is being learned. The children in second grade were beginning to look for patterns in what they learned. The children had studied the panda before studying the tiger, and some noticed that the tiger, like the panda, is a non-social animal, and they were interested in finding out why. The teacher and librarian provided opportunities for students to decide what information to select and how to organize it; they also supported investigation in response to students' questions.

Appendix D

Planning for Inquiry

Jean Donham

T he teacher and the library media specialist collaboratively plan for inquiry. The information search process provides a scaffold for this planning and for the roles that each partner will play. Figure A-3 on page 80 reminds each partner of skills/tasks at each stage of the process. As the unit is planned, these reminders guide what must be taught or what activities will occur as the process proceeds. During the planning meeting, the teacher and library media specialist make notes for each of these skills/tasks regarding how they will be addressed in this particular unit.

PLANNING FOR INQUIRY

Unit Topic:_____

Initiating the Inquiry	
Teacher	**Library Media Specialist**
Student expectations:	
Experiences for generating inquiry	Resources for building background/exploration
Selecting a Topic	
Criteria for acceptable topics	Availability of resources
Exploring Information	
Reading to become informed	Locating relevant information
Forming a Focus	
Reading for themes	Generating researchable questions on the focused topic
Collecting Information	
Reading for meaning	Selecting information resources
Taking and organizing notes	Applying search strategies for focused topic
	Generating a bibliography
Presenting Results	
Planning and organizing the final product	Using tools to create presentation, e.g., computer applications
Assessing the Process	
Student learning about the topic	Student learning about the research process

FIGURE A-3

For Further Reading

While many references related to inquiry-based learning are available in the literature, the following brief list of selections provides additional examples and insights into the information search process, constructivism, and inquiry, particularly as these principles relate to one another. This is by no means an exhaustive list, but it provides ideas for additional resources to extend familiarity with these practices.

Books

Harvey, Stephanie, and Anne Goudvis. *Strategies that Work: Teaching Comprehension to Enhance Understanding.* Stenhouse Publishers, 2000.

A constructivist approach to reading comprehension characterizes this work. The strategies described here fit well in an inquiry-based learning context.

Lieberman, Ann, and Lynne Miller. *Teachers—Transforming Their World and Their Work.* Reston, VA: ASCD, 1999.

The importance of facilitating teacher transformation in the adoption of educational reform frames this work.

Oldfather, Penny. *Learning Through Children's Eyes: Social Constructivism and the Desire to Learn.* Washington, DC: American Psychological Association, June 1999.

This practical handbook presents the principles of constructivism and concrete advice and examples for implementing these principles in the classroom.

Thomas, Nancy P. *Information Literacy and Information Skills Instruction: Applying Research to Practice in the School Library Media Center.* Englewood, CO: Libraries Unlimited, 1999.

With references to the research on information seeking, this work synthesizes trends in information literacy and describes implementation of the research in library media instruction programs.

Zweizig, Douglas L., and Diane McAfee Hopkins. *Lessons from Library Power: Enriching Teaching and Learning*. Englewood, CO: Libraries Unlimited, 1999.

The authors provide background information on the Library Power initiative, report on research findings from the project, and discuss current and future implications of the Library Power evaluation. Research findings are reported in chapters organized around the following categories: collections, access to and use of library resources, collaboration, curriculum, instruction, school reform, professional development, and institutionalization.

Articles

Bishop, Kay, "The research processes of gifted students: A case study." *Gifted Child Quarterly*. (Winter 2000): 54-64.

The researcher investigated the research processes of ten gifted, junior-high students. Students experienced the most difficulty in exploring and forming a focus. The author provides recommendations related to producing more authentic student learning experiences from independent research projects.

Keedy, J. L., and C. M. Achilles. "The need for school-constructed theories in practice in U.S. school restructuring." *Journal of Educational Administration* 35(2) (1997): 102-121.

Keedy and Achilles argue that school reforms related to teaching for understanding cannot occur without school staffs reconceptualizing the norms of instruction. Such changes require that school staffs engage in reflection about their work and design their own theories in practice. This process involves two steps: (1) critical inquiry into current practice and desired outcomes, and (2) monitoring the change process to ensure progress toward consensus and accomplishment of the desired outcomes.

Pappas, Marjorie L. "Managing the inquiry learning environment." *School Library Media Activities Monthly* (March 2000): 27-30, 36.

The writer discusses inquiry-learning advice for changing from a traditional pedagogical approach to inquiry.

Pataray-Ching, Jann, and Deborah Kavanaugh-Anderson, "Supporting learner-generated inquiries." *The Educational Forum* (Fall 1999): 58-66.

A case study of a curriculum-as-inquiry model describes a learner-generated inquiry process where students became more focused and productive, developed more ownership of their learning, and spent more time exploring their studies both inside and outside the classroom.

Showers, B., and B. Joyce. "The evolution of peer coaching." *Educational Leadership* 53 (6) (1996): 12-16.

Showers and Joyce examine the history of peer coaching, describe changes in coaching practice, and make recommendations for its future. Consultants assisting in the implementation of innovation in schools have found that for increased success, all teachers must agree to be members of peer coaching study teams and to omit verbal feedback. This research suggests that when "coaching" is seen as collaborative teamwork, teacher learning is enhanced and extended in unforeseen ways.

Tastad, Shirley, and Norma Decker Collins. "Teaching the information skills process and the writing process: Bridging the gap." *School Library Media Quarterly* (Spring 1997): 167-169.

In this research study, the authors suggest that the efforts of middle-school teachers to use a writing center were not successful because a constructivist philosophy did not support a process approach to teaching writing. The researchers note that a constructivist philosophy of learning is crucial to implementing a process approach to teaching. Findings support earlier studies conducted by Carol Kuhlthau.

About the Authors

Jean Donham directs the library at Cornell College in Mount Vernon, Iowa. Previously, she was associate professor at the University of Iowa School of Library and Information Science, where she taught courses in school librarianship. Earlier, Dr. Donham served as District Coordinator of the library media program for the Iowa City (Iowa) Community Schools. Her publishing and research interests are in flexible scheduling, school library media management, and teacher-library media specialist collaboration. She served as a case study researcher for the Library Power Evaluation Project. She is the author of *Enhancing Teaching and Learning: A Leadership Guide for School Library Media Specialists.*

Kay Bishop is an associate professor in the School of Library and Information Science at the University of South Florida, where she teaches courses in school media and youth services. She also has been on the faculties of the University of Kentucky, the University of Southern Mississippi, and Murray State University and has had 20 years of experience as a school library media specialist in public and private schools. Dr. Bishop has conducted research on the roles of a school media specialist in a literature-based reading program, the reviewing of children's books, gender and ethnic bias in juvenile computer books, the research processes of gifted students, the impact of technology on school media centers, and the programs and strategies that attract young people to public libraries. She served as a case study researcher for the National Program Evaluation of Library Power. She is actively involved in school media and youth services professional organizations and has made presentations at state, national, and international conferences.

Carol Kuhlthau is Professor and Chair of the Library and Information Science Department and Director of the MLS program in the School of Communication, Information and Library Studies at Rutgers University in New Brunswick, New Jersey. Known for her research into the user's perspective of the information search process, she has written numerous papers, articles, and books, including *Seeking Meaning: a Process Approach to Library and Information Services* and *Teaching the Library Research Process*. She is a frequent presenter on information literacy and topics related to her research. Kuhlthau is a recipient of the American Library Association's Jesse Shera Research Award, the ACRL Miriam Dudley Bibliographic Instruction Award, and the AASL Distinguished Service Award.

Dianne Oberg is Professor and Chair of the Department of Elementary Education at the University of Alberta, Edmonton, Alberta, Canada. Her teaching areas include resource-based teaching and learning, school library program development, and school library collection development. Her research work focuses on teachers' use of libraries, the implementation and evaluation of school library programs, and the use of the Internet in schools. She has conducted studies related to the role of the principal and the role of the teacher-librarian in program implementation. She has been involved as an individual evaluator and as a member of an evaluation team, assessing school library programs at the school and district level since 1987. She was a case study researcher for the National Program Evaluation of Library Power. Dr. Oberg has had many years of experience as a classroom teacher and as a teacher-librarian in elementary and secondary schools, and she has been actively involved in school library association work from the local to the international level. She is the editor of the international refereed journal, *School Libraries Worldwide*.

Index

information search process (ISP) model, viii, 8, 65, 67, 71, 80
    as affective gauge, 5–6, 17, 20, 21, 50
    as common lexicon, 22–23
    as curricular scaffold, 17–21, 30, 79
    as student guide, 24–27, 73–75
    for monitoring student progress, 27–28
    functions of, 16–17, 28
    planning for inquiry and, 79–80
    stages of, 5–7, 16–17, 50–51
    see also Kuhlthau, Carol Collier
inquiry-based learning, vi–viii, 2, 7–11, 67–68, 78, 82
    constructivist theory and, 1–4
    enablers of, 10, 28, 30
    implementation of, 8–10, 48–55, 65
    in information-age school, 10–11
    in information-rich environment, 5
    inhibitors of, 10
    stages in, 5–7
    vs. project-centered approach, 9, 54
interdisciplinary units, 49, 52–54, 60–62, 65
Invitations: Changing as Teachers and Learners K–12 (Routman), 37, 41

Joyce, B. 43, 83

Kelly, George, 3
Kingston Elementary School, 13–30
    description of, 13–16
    staff development in, 14–16, 30
    use of information search process model, 16–29
Kuhlthau, Carol Collier, iii, vi, 1, 16–17, 20–22, 24–25, 49, 54, 69, 71, 72, 83, 85
    see also information search process (ISP) model
KWL, 49, 73–74

"Library Lab," 15 library media center facilities, viii, 33, 55–56, 65
Library Media Specialists
    collaboration with teachers, 8, 14, 23, 48–51, 53–54, 61, 66, 67
    perceptions of learning and, 7–8
    roles of, vii, 5, 8, 14, 45, 36–37, 55, 64, 68, 80
Library Power, vi, 7, 69–72, 82
    assessment of student learning, 70–71
    data analysis and, 71–72
    effects of, 11, 33, 34, 62–64
    purpose, 14
    research methods, 69–70
The Lily Cupboard: A Story of the Holocaust (Oppenheim), 19

matrix
    see curriculum mapping McCarthy, S. J., 35
models
    see information search process (ISP)
model multiple intelligences, 4

My Best Friend (Hutchins), 38

Newmann, Fred M., 70
normative thinking, 35, 40, 68

Oberg, Dianne, iii, iv, 31, 76, 85